Ghost Stories of
Newfoundland and Labrador

EDWARD BUTTS

GHOST STORIES OF NEWFOUNDLAND AND LABRADOR

DUNDURN PRESS
TORONTO

Editor: Nicole Chaplin
Design: Courtney Horner
Printer: Webcom

Library and Archives Canada Cataloguing in Publication

Butts, Edward, 1951-
    Ghost stories of Newfoundland and Labrador / by Edward Butts.

Issued also in an electronic format.
ISBN 978-1-55488-785-9

    1. Ghosts--Newfoundland and Labrador. 2. Haunted places--Newfoundland and Labrador. I. Title.

BF1472.C3B88 2010   133.109718   C2010-902416-8

1   2   3   4   5   14   13   12   11   10

We acknowledge the support of the **Canada Council for the Arts** and the **Ontario Arts Council** for our publishing program. We also acknowledge the financial support of the **Government of Canada** through the **Canada Book Fund** and **The Association for the Export of Canadian Books**, and the **Government of Ontario** through the **Ontario Book Publishers Tax Credit program**, and the **Ontario Media Development Corporation**.

Care has been taken to trace the ownership of copyright materials used in this book. The author and the publisher welcome any information enabling them to rectify any references or credits in subsequent editions.

J. Kirk Howard, President

Published by Dundurn Press
Printed and bound in Canada.

www.dundurn.com

Dundurn Press	Gazelle Book Services Limited	Dundurn Press
3 Church Street, Suite 500	White Cross Mills	2250 Military Road
Toronto, Ontario, Canada	High Town, Lancaster, England	Tonawanda, NY
M5E 1M2	LA1 4XS	U.S.A. 14150

In memory of my grandparents,
John Butts of Harbour Grace and Mary Nugent of Kelligrews

Table of Contents

Acknowledgements   11

Introduction   13

Q & A With Diana Leadbeater   15

Oft Told Tales: St. John's   24

     The Ghosts of Signal Hill   24

     The Headless Captain   27

     The Ghost of Catherine Snow   29

     The Duelist's Ghost   30

     The Haunted Hotel Room   33

     The Missing Gravestone   35

     The Cry of the Banshee   36

     Cold Fire   38

     A Nightmare on Gower Street   39

Case Files: St. John's   41

     The Knights of Columbus Fire   41

     The Ghost Next Door   43

     Q & A With Gene Browne   47

     Gene Browne's Haunted House   52

Oft Told Tales: Literature and Folklore   57

     The Oral Tradition   57

Jack the Sailor   57

Brave Jack and the Ghosts   60

A Ghostly Ballad   64

Fair Marjorie's Ghost   64

Mischievous Fairies   65

Case Files: The Old Hag   67

Dead Lady and the Night Hag   71

Gene Browne's Old Hag   74

Tom's Story   75

It Didn't Like Me   76

Judy's Story   77

Just the Hag, Not My Ghost   79

A Scratching Noise   80

Courtney's Story   81

Mysteries of the Sea   83

The Ghostly Crew of the *Charles Haskell*   83

The Ghost That Wasn't   88

Tale of a Haunted Ship   92

Samson's Island Ghost   94

A Mystery of the Gulf   96

Harry Smith of the *Falcon*   101

The Wreck of the *Ella M. Rudolf*   102

"How True!"   104

Ghosts of HMS *Harpooner*   104

The Keys   106

The Dower Mystery   108

The Wrecker   109

The Phantom Galley   110

The Ghost Light of Trinity   111

Ghosts on the Ice   113

X Marks the Spot   119

Guardians of Pirate Treasure   119

Torbay's Treasure Cove   122
The Ghosts of Shoal Bay   124
The Ghosts of Copper Island   127
The Ghosts of Kelly's Island   129
The Ghosts of Chapel Cove Pond   131
The Treasures of Captain Kidd   133

Oft Told Tales: Around the Island   136
The Ghost Train of Buchans   136
Lost in the Woods   137
The Black Stag   138
The Ghost of Clarke's Beach   140
The Ghost of Holyrood   141
The Corpse Light of Harbour Grace   142
Unless He Went Down Dead   144
The Town That Disappeared   147
Disaster at Dead Man's Gulch   148

Case Files: Around the Island   152
Bad Dreams in the Basement   152
Knitting Needles and a Corduroy Jacket   155
The Click of Knitting Needles   156
The Man in the Corduroy Jacket   157
Dark Shadows   159
Gran's Sewing Machine   161
I Thought the Door Got Hit With a Sledgehammer   162
I Just Come by to Say Goodbye   164
Two Ghost Stories   165
The Fishing Trip   166
The Helpful Ghost   168
Three Mystic Experiences   170
A Picture of Dad   170
A Paper Cross   171
One Single Red Rose   172
I Refused to Be Scared of My House   172

That Was Mother   178

The Flatrock Fires   180

The Whole House Was Haunted   182

A Near Trip to Heaven   186

Oft Told Tales: Labrador   189

The Mysterious Trapper of Labrador   189

The Mystery of Sam Croucher's Gold   192

Case Files: Ghosts of Labrador   194

Courtney's Story: Slamming Doors   194

Jenny's Story: The Man Behind the Furnace   196

Amanda's Story: Indian Graves   197

Pamela's Story: "This is Really Beginning to Scare Me"   198

Olive's Story: "I Could See Right Through Him"   199

Cherie's Story: Try to Explain That   200

Jennifer's Story: A Big Bang   201

Jody's Story: I Hate That House   202

Matt's Story: I Got a Little Freaked   203

Odd Tales   205

A Problematic Dream   205

Scared to Death   208

Dead Men Can Advance No Farther   211

Bibliography   217

Acknowledgements

I could not have completed this book without the help and contributions of many people. I must first thank Michael Carroll and Kirk Howard of Dundurn Press for giving me the opportunity to work on this fascinating project, and Nicole Chaplin for her editorial assistance. I am indebted to John Robert Colombo, Canada's greatest collector of ghost stories, for his contributions and for his many excellent books. I had the good fortune to meet — online at least — Diana Leadbeater of the Newfoundland Paranormal Society, Gene Browne of the Newfoundland Paranormal Investigation group, and Matt Massie and Frank Pottle of the Ghosts of Labrador group. They made invaluable contributions to this book, and were of inestimable help when I was getting started with my research. I owe thanks to author Jack Fitzgerald, a Newfoundland icon whose books on everything from ghosts to criminals I highly recommend.

My request for personal stories about experiences with ghosts and the infamous Old Hag reached people in communities across the province, and even in other parts of Canada, thanks to Shawn Tetford, the Executive Director of Newfoundland and Labrador Public Libraries. Thanks to all of the Newfoundland and Labrador newspapers that kindly ran my letter to the editor, as well as CBC Radio in Grand Falls, for which I was interviewed about the project. For stories that I received by email and by post, I thank Bernard Maloney, Rita Alexander, W. Rex Stirling, Judy Newhook, J.Y. Ferguson, Sean Clarke, and Donna Barr. My gratitude also goes to all the people who answered my request for stories, but who wish to remain anonymous. I am grateful for their compelling accounts, and for their trust. My thanks to Drew MacGillivray for his perspective on the Old Hag. Finally, I thank Wayne Butt and David Liverman for their help with photographs, Michelle Blackman for her drawing of the Old Hag, and once again the staff at the Guelph, Ontario, Public Library.

Introduction

When Michael Carroll, the editorial director of Dundurn Press, asked me if I would like to write a book about Newfoundland and Labrador ghost stories, I immediately said yes. The project appealed to me for several reasons: I have always loved storytelling, and I was very aware of the rich tradition of storytelling that still exists in Newfoundland and Labrador. I don't necessarily mean storytelling as it is done on stage by a gifted raconteur, although that is certainly wonderful when it is done well. Rather, I mean the kind of storytelling that goes on in a home, usually in the kitchen, at a gathering of family and friends. There is no distraction from the television or recorded music — just people sharing stories. As a boy I had first hand exposure to it through my paternal grandfather, a native-born Newfoundlander.

While I have lived most of my life in Ontario, I always knew that Newfoundland is a treasure trove of stories, both written and oral. The stock of tales has been building up for some five hundred years. Excluding the folk tales of First Nations, that is longer than in any other part of Canada and the number continues to grow.

I have always been intrigued by stories about ghosts and the supernatural. I have never seen a ghost, nor have I ever had a paranormal experience — at least, not that I have been aware of — but I have known many people, including family members, who say that they have. With few exceptions, I accept that these people have indeed experienced *something* that seems to defy logical explanation. I cannot say for certain that ghosts exist, but I would not flatly deny their existence.

Because of Newfoundland and Labrador's maritime history, many of the traditional ghost stories involve pirates and buried treasure. Those tales are well represented here, along with those involving shipwrecks, sealing disasters, and strange events at sea. Among the ghostly entries from Newfoundland folklore are an old ballad, and two "Jack Tales," adapted from versions in *The Book of Newfoundland*.

In addition to the traditional ghost stories that the people of Newfoundland and Labrador have been telling for generations, I thought it would be interesting to include personal accounts from people who have had paranormal experiences. This presented me with a new challenge: to research my previous books, I used archival records, long forgotten newspaper articles, and books so long out of print that it sometimes required serious detective work to track them down. This time, I would somehow have to reach out to total strangers halfway across Canada and ask them to share stories, on a somewhat intimate topic, with a writer in Guelph, Ontario.

By means of a letter to the editor published in newspapers across Newfoundland and Labrador, a notice posted in public libraries throughout the province, a CBC radio interview, as well as appeals that went out via email, Facebook, and YouTube, I managed to reach people who were interested in sharing their stories. Some even sent me their stories by handwritten letters.

Some of the stories with which people entrusted me are truly unnerving. Others tell of rather beautiful encounters with deceased loved ones. Then there are the ones that involve that unique Newfoundland creature of the night, the Old Hag.

Some of the people who contributed stories requested that I not include their names, and I have respected their wishes. Also, out of respect for people's privacy, I have not given the addresses of houses in which these ghostly encounters occurred. I've kept the stories as close to the original as they have been written, only making corrections in grammar or structure in places where the text might otherwise have been confusing. Warning! Some stories might make readers want to keep a light on at night.

Q & A With Diana Leadbeater

The Newfoundland
Paranormal Society

*Researching, Archiving,
Promoting, Helping*

Logo of the Newfoundland Paranormal Society.

Diana Leadbeater is a founder of the Newfoundland Paranormal Society, based in St. John's. She feels that in addition to its wealth of history and culture, Newfoundland also has an intriguing record of paranormal events that deserve to be researched and documented. As Diana states on the NPS website, "If you're ever lucky enough to see my book collection, you will see that it is 95% ghost and paranormal related." The views she states here, she says, "are only my opinions and knowledge. Some other members might have different views."

Name of Organization: Newfoundland Paranormal Society (NPS)
Date Founded: NPS founded October 2009
Founder: NPS-founder is Diana Leadbeater, co-founder is Grace Shears.
Favourite Newfoundland and Labrador Haunt: The Masonic Temple.
Website: *sites.google.com/site/newfoundlandparanormalsociety/Home*

Mission: Created in 2009, the Newfoundland Paranormal Society is made up of not-for-profit investigators, private researchers, and paranormal enthusiasts dedicated to researching and documenting the paranormal history and events occurring in Newfoundland. The goal of the society is to be an official place where various investigative and interest groups can come together to provide greater public access to their information and services.

The Newfoundland Paranormal Society was founded with the intention of being a reliable resource for anyone seeking knowledge and understanding of the paranormal and helping those individuals, families, or businesses that may be experiencing phenomena that they do not understand.

Q: Why is the Masonic Temple your favourite haunt?

A: It is my favourite haunt because of the history of the building. The building itself is over one hundred years old and has only ever been under control by the masons. It is only recently due to costs that they had to give it up. The history is also interesting, the fact that many of the rooms upstairs women and general public have never been allowed in due to mason rules. It is also a very huge building with many small and hidden rooms.

The haunting itself is that there are so many reported paranormal events there, ranging from intelligent haunting to residual. They have heard big band music, heard people talking, and seen possible shadow people.

Q: How long have you been investigating the paranormal?

A: I have been interested all my life and for the last five years have been doing my own investigating.

Q: When did your interest begin?

A: Funny thing is that I can't really remember when my interest began. As far back as I can remember I've always been interested.

Q: How did that interest progress?

A: It started as just reading as many ghost stories as I could, to now running the NPS, being a member of NPI, and also [being] the Newfoundland representative for International Paranormal Investigators.

Q: Would you say that you take a skeptical approach to a new investigation?

A: I take a balanced approach to investigations. I need go in as neither a skeptic nor a believer. I have a scientific academic background, and I use this to base my investigations on.

Q: What are some of the explanations you've found to what appear to be paranormal phenomena?

A: The constantly occurring classic one is the sounds of banging and noises in the walls which turn out to be mice or pipes that were not fastened to the walls.

Q: Could a psychic give you direction in an investigation?

A: I would not say no, but at the same time I would not put much weight into it nor base my entire investigation on it.

Q: What equipment do you use to investigate?

A: For modern equipment I use digital voice recorders, temperature guns, digital video cameras, and infrared cameras. I also use other non-traditional equipment such as paper and pen, trigger objects, talcum powder or flour, balls, level, tissue paper, matches, etc.

Q: What are "trigger objects"?

A: Trigger objects are objects that someone might have used in real life or something of significance or interest to them. For example, religious people in life might touch or move a cross or some other religious object placed in the room. Using a ball or toy might help bring out action from a child ghost. A trigger object would be anything (physical, music, etc.) that might get a reaction from the reported ghost or stimulate the environment.

Q: How do you talk to a spirit?

A: The same way I talk to a living person. I tend to speak with respect and not use the agitation method so many others do. I am also very careful to word my questions in a way that any possible answer can only mean one thing. The problem with many teams is that they ask a question, get a bang, and assume it answered. However the way they asked the question, the bang could have meant a yes or a no.

Q: Are there certain criteria that must be met before you agree to an investigation?

A: Yes. NPS has a long list of requirements and criteria that should be met before agreeing to an investigation. For example, we must be able to have an interview with the client to get as much information as we can and ascertain if the area is safe enough to investigate.

Q: What conditions must a potential client meet to convince you to take a case?

A: We do not have strict conditions laid out but the decision is done based on the initial client information collected and the personal interviews. The main thing is, does the client have the permission or can get permission for the team to investigate.

Q: Do your clients ask for evidence, or do they want you to disprove a paranormal existence in their home or business to put them at ease?

A: We get a mix of both. However, we express that we are there to neither prove nor disprove. We will provide assistance to put their minds at ease if it is really bothering them.

Q: Is your primary mission to find answers regarding the existence of ghosts, or to help people who are living with them?

A: Primary mission is twofold: (1) to collect as much data as we can regarding possible existence of ghosts; and (2) to provide information to the general public about the paranormal world.

Q: Are the ghost hunting programs on TV very accurate?

A: Very few of them are, actually. Many are over dramatized in order to grab the audiences' attention. Very few cases ever have anything occur or, if there is, then the occurrences are not as grand as many of those episodes are.

Q: What do you see in the future for your organization?
A: To become a central hub to assist in promoting all paranormal teams and issues across Newfoundland.

Q: How do you decide who will go on an investigation with you?
A: Only members selected and screened to be on the team can go: we do not take random people. Each team member goes through training before going on an investigation. It also depends on the size of the site: bigger sites require more investigators, smaller sites you need to limit.

Q: What type of person is best suited for this work?
A: One with an open mind who thinks of various possibilities, who is not overly religious, and doesn't have a bias of some fashion.

Q: You say each team member goes through training. What sort of training?
A: They are given extensive training on how to use the various kinds of equipment. This is to make sure they are using it right, and know what can go wrong that will cause fake paranormal readings. They also undergo training on safety procedures to follow, procedures to follow when filling out investigation paperwork, and how to act on an investigation. We do not give someone a recorder and throw them into a room. They need to know how to act and behave to best catch possible evidence.

When I talk about how to behave, they need to understand that sound carries and they need to walk carefully. If they make a noise themselves, they need to make notice of that at the time on the voice recorder. They also need to be taught that they don't always have to be walking, but can sit down, as well as how to behave if something paranormal does happen to them. They need to be taught how to handle digital recorders in order to not contaminate evidence with actions they did themselves. We do not want them to freak out or get overly excited. One has to think calmly and rationally to go after what just happened, and determine why it did.

Q: Do you think a paranormal investigation could result in a scientific breakthrough?

A: Not in the way it is all currently done. Being in a scientific academic position, I know the scientific world would not accept any evidence unless it can be duplicated and pass the current set scientific method. Also, no one right now even knows if the equipment we are using actually registers what we think it does. For all we know, what we are registering could be something completely unknown and unrelated to what we think are ghosts. Since we don't have a true ghost that we can test the equipment on, we can't say it is doing what we think it is doing.

Q: Have you ever felt you were in danger during an investigation?

A: No.

Q: What protective measures do you take?

A: Proper safety measures such as making sure the area is safe to be in, wearing proper masks, having safety gear if the location is not fully safe to normally be in.

Q: Do you learn everything you can about a location before you actually go there?

A: Yes. It would be illogical and unsafe not to.

Q: What about cases where you don't find anything?

A: Just because you don't find anything can mean two things: (1) there is nothing there; (2) there is something there but just not at the time we were investigating. Too many groups only go once to a place and decide on what they find. To really get a good understanding you need long term repeat investigations to collect data.

Q: What sort of evidence do you look for?

A: Physical evidence that can be scrutinized and evaluated using accepted scientific methods.

Q: What are the different kinds of hauntings?

A: If you break it down into broad categories there are residual, intellectual, and poltergeist haunting.

Q: Can you define residual, intellectual, and poltergeist hauntings?

A: Residual haunting is like a tape or video player. It occurs exactly the same, and possibly at the same time. Like a video tape recording an event and then playing it over and over. There is no intelligence there. For example, when people hear music playing, it usually is residual; it's energy that's been caught or engrained in the building, and plays out, over and over.

An intellectual haunting is interactive. There is an intelligence behind it, and it will interact with people. An intellectual haunting, for example, is the typical ghost where it responds to your questions. It is like you are interacting with a real live person.

Poltergeist haunting is usually difficult to figure out. In this case there is usually knocking and tapping noises, sounds with no visible cause, disturbance of stationary objects like household objects and furniture, doors slamming, lights turning on and off, fires breaking out, objects moving and being thrown, people being physically attacked, and more. Many of these do overlap with intellectual and residual haunting. The theory here that makes it different is that it is not caused by a spirit or is residual.

The theory is that poltergeist hauntings are caused by a real life person in the household, known as the "human agent." This human agent is typically an adolescent who is undergoing puberty, and is troubled emotionally; however, this is not always the case. It is speculated that in these cases the person has psychokinesis (PK), which is the ability to move things by manipulating energy generated by their brain. Most of the time this ability is not known to the individual, nor do they know they are causing the poltergeist activity.

There is much debate within the paranormal community on what exactly is the cause of poltergeist activity. The main way to make the difference is that it does not occur when the human agent is not in the location, but returns once they do so, or follows them to the new location they are at.

Q: What can bring an entity, friendly or unfriendly, into a building?

A: Many different things can, actually. Hypotheses are many in that they can be attracted/attached to an individual or an item, the building was built using pieces of some other building to which the entity was attached/living in, someone brought back a rock or item from a reported haunted location, they are attached to the land the building is built on, the building is connected or close to another place the entity lived or died in, or someone opened a gate by accident or on purpose.

Q: What do you mean by a "gate"?

A: A gate is also referred to as a portal. It is a connection between our world and the possible spirit world. It is a connection point that allows spirits to come over into the real world and/or go back and forth between the two.

The theory is that there are natural gates that occur. However, when people play around with Ouija boards or do things they don't fully understand, they can make these gates. The Ouija board is supposed to work by being a window to the spirit world. However, when used wrong, it can become a gate. As a window, the spirit can only communicate. But when it becomes a gate, it can then come into the person's house in the real world.

All paranormal theories that people talk about are really only hypotheses. Nothing can be theory since there is no way to scientifically prove it. The theory of relativity can be proved; the theory of haunting can't be. As well, nobody can say they are an expert, because you can't fully understand anything if it can't be tested and proven over and over again. One may be very knowledgeable in the area, but they can't be an expert.

Q: Are Ouija boards dangerous?

A: Depends on if you believe that they are actually a portal or not. In my opinion they are as dangerous as a monopoly board. It is the mind frame of the person using it that is dangerous. It is possible that it is not the board itself that opens a gateway but the person's behaviour or themselves that becomes the gateway.

Q: Are people's attitudes toward the paranormal changing?

A: Attitudes have been changing across the century. It comes and goes on if it is popular or not.

Oft Told Tales: St John's

The Ghosts of Signal Hill

Signal Hill, the massive rock formation that rises above St. John's, is said to be a very haunted place. Small wonder, because over the centuries this landmark has seen its share of violence, misery, and death. Given the claim that St. John's is one of the most haunted cities in North America, it would be strange if Signal Hill did *not* have ghosts.

In the mid eighteenth century, a promontory on Signal Hill became the site of a gibbet. This was a structure that resembled a gallows pole, but was used to display the bodies of executed criminals. In those days people were "hanged by the neck until dead" not only for major crimes, like murder and rape, but also for petty theft, forgery, and rustling cattle or pigs. After the execution, the body was coated with tar and hung from a gibbet as a grim warning to others. Whatever was left by the carrion birds was eventually tossed into Deadman's Pond below Signal Hill. The promontory on which the gibbet was erected became known as Gibbet Hill.

In 1762, Signal Hill was the scene of the final battle of the Seven Years War between the French and the British. The clash was a minor one by the standards of the time, but there were casualties before the French finally surrendered. When the victorious British realized the military importance of Signal Hill, they built fortifications there.

It was a fact of life in the eighteenth and nineteenth centuries that a common soldier was more likely to die from disease than from battle wounds. This was very true for the redcoat troops stationed at Signal

In this sketch from 1851, Gibbett Hill can be seen to the right in the background. The bodies of executed criminals were hung there as a warning to others. Their remains were eventually dumped in Deadman's Pond.

Hill. Indeed, some considered it the most miserable outpost in the British Empire.

Crowded into poorly constructed barracks that were exposed to the elements, the men were almost always cold. Their quarters were damp and verminous. Sanitation was primitive. Epidemics swept through the ranks, and there was little the army doctors could do for the sick men. Long after the final battle had been fought, Signal Hill became the last post for many soldiers.

In 1847 a fire destroyed the St. John's courthouse and jail. A barracks on Signal Hill was made into a prison; it was in operation for twelve years. The prison was crowded, and for most of those locked up there, conditions were harsh.

Between 1879 and 1920, whenever epidemics struck St. John's, Signal Hill was used as an isolation ward for the sick. Victims of smallpox, cholera, diphtheria, typhus, and tuberculosis were all brought up to the drafty old barracks on the hill. Many of them died, and quite possibly their unhappy spirits joined those already haunting Signal Hill.

The Cabot Tower on Signal Hill is said to be haunted by the ghost of a woman whose baby died in her arms.

One of the most enduring Signal Hill ghost stories is that of a baby that died in its mother's arms. According to a report written in 1842, the mother was sitting in a rocking chair in a room heated by a fireplace. Because of poor ventilation, the room would become very smoky, and the mother would have to open a window from time to time to clear the air. But then the room would get cold, and she would have to close the window again. She finally fell asleep while the window was closed. She awoke, coughing, in a smoke-filled room, to find that the child in her arms had died from smoke inhalation. Her ghost is now said to sit in Signal Hill's Cabot Tower every night, rocking in a chair and wailing over the lost baby.

Another Signal Hill ghost is that of a woman whose husband went away with the Newfoundland Regiment to fight in the First World War. In 1918, when a troop ship brought the men back, all of their mothers, sweethearts, and wives were waiting for them on the dock. The woman in question was there with her child. Sadly, she was among the women whose men did not return. Now, every night the ghosts of the woman and child fly across Signal Hill in search of the fallen soldier.

Besides being a dumping ground for corpses from Gibbet Hill, Deadman's Pond is also the site of several drownings. Among the victims were two girls who, in 1869, went through the ice while skating. Frederick Carter Jr., the son of Newfoundland's premier, Sir Frederick Carter, made a heroic effort to save them. All three died. Deadman's Pond is also said to be the hiding place of pirate treasure, and therefore would have resident pirate ghosts. According to legend, the pond is bottomless. From Deadman's Pond up to Gibbet Hill, it seems there is hardly a spot on craggy Signal Hill that is not haunted.

The Headless Captain

Of all the apparitions that have found their way into lore, legend, and literature, perhaps none would be more unnerving than a headless ghost. The spectre of Anne Boleyn, King Henry VIII's unlucky second wife, who was decapitated for her alleged infidelity, is said to roam the Tower of London with, as the old song says, "her head tucked underneath her arm." In Washington Irving's classic short story "The Legend of Sleepy Hollow," the Headless Horseman terrifies poor Ichabod Crane. St. John's also has a legendary headless ghost.

In 1745 a man named Samuel Pettyham rented a St. John's house that had once been the home of a beautiful woman who was part of a tragic love triangle. Pettyham knew nothing of the building's history or its former occupant. However, soon after he moved in, he was disturbed at night when the latches of the front and back doors began mysteriously lifting, as though someone was trying to gain entry. He would throw the door open, expecting to confront the would-be intruder, only to find no one there.

Pettyham found this annoying, but he likely put it down as the work of pranksters. The nightly jiggling of the door latches certainly wasn't enough to make him want to move to new quarters. He simply ensured that his doors were well-bolted at night to discourage thieves. Then, one night, Pettyham saw something that frightened the wits out of him.

He had been visiting a friend, and was returning home late. As he walked along the street toward his residence, Pettyham saw what appeared to be a glowing light in the shadows. His first thought was that it must be someone with a torch. He got closer, and then saw the figure of a tall man silhouetted in the moonlight. The man was standing in front of Pettyham's house. Due to the lateness of the hour, the street was otherwise deserted. Most decent, law-abiding people were home in their beds. Pettyham thought that this might be the scoundrel who'd been trying to get into his house.

He strode forward quickly, prepared to confront the knave and demand to know what he was up to. But Pettyham had taken but a few steps when he suddenly stopped, frozen in his tracks with fear. The tall figure standing in the street in front of him was indeed that of a man — with no head!

Pettyham took a few unsteady steps backwards, wide-eyed at the sight of the thing in front of him. Then he turned and ran. He rounded a corner, and saw a light in the window of a boarding house. Afraid that the headless man might be right behind him, Pettyham pounded on the boarding house door. When the landlord opened it, Pettyham begged the man to let him in.

Once he was inside, with the door closed and locked behind him, Pettyham calmed down enough to tell the landlord what had happened. He was afraid that the man would think he was drunk or crazy. Instead, the landlord listened to him patiently, and told him the story of the house in which he'd been living.

The beautiful woman who had once resided in Pettyham's home had two lovers. One was a man who lived in St. John's. The other was a tall, dashing English sea captain who would stay with her whenever his ship put in at St. John's. The woman tried to keep her relationship with one lover secret from the other. But in a small community like St. John's, where everybody knew everybody else's business, that was next to impossible.

The lover who resided in St. John's found out about the English sea captain and the woman he'd thought was his own ladylove. He was consumed with jealousy. There was nothing else he could do, he thought, but murder the interfering captain.

The next time the captain visited the woman's house, the jealous lover was outside, lurking in the shadows of the night. He had rage in his heart and a sword in his hand. His fury grew as he thought of the woman he loved in the arms of another man.

When the unsuspecting captain came out of the house, the assassin struck quickly. Attacking from behind, with one stroke of his sword he cut off the captain's head. As the body collapsed in a pool of blood, and the head rolled in the street, the killer fled. He disappeared from St. John's, and was never apprehended.

The landlord told Pettyham that other people had seen that headless ghost. They had no doubt that it was the murdered English captain. But did the ghost haunt that street because it longed for the love of the beautiful woman, or was it searching for the unpunished killer? As for Samuel Pettyham, he made arrangements for new living quarters, and never set foot in that house again.

The Ghost of Catherine Snow

On the night of August 31, 1833, John Snow of Salmon Cove, Port de Grave, was murdered. The killers were Arthur Spring, Snow's bonded servant; and Tobias Manderville, who was a cousin of Snow's wife, Catherine. After shooting Snow, they dumped his body at sea (it was never recovered), and then arranged the crime scene to make it appear that Snow had been a robbery victim.

Spring and Mandeville were found out, however, and Spring confessed. He said that Mrs. Snow was behind the murder plot. Catherine and Mandeville were lovers, said Spring. She wanted her husband dead so she and Mandeville could get married and go away together.

In January 1834, all three were tried in St. John's for murder, and found guilty. Spring and Mandeville were hanged, and their bodies were gibbeted. But Catherine's execution had to be postponed because she was pregnant.

For the next few months Catherine Snow was kept in the St. John's jail, awaiting the birth of her child and her own death. All the while, she pleaded her innocence. Many people in Newfoundland supported her cause, especially since Arthur Spring had retracted his claim that she had been involved in the murder conspiracy. But the magistrate who condemned her would not be moved. In July, shortly after her baby was born, Catherine was hanged. The execution took place outside the old St. John's courthouse, just east of the site of the present courthouse on Duckworth Street. Catherine protested her innocence to the very end. The local Roman Catholic clergy did not believe Catherine's guilt had been proven in court, so they allowed her body to be interred in consecrated ground in the Catholic cemetery at the bottom of Long's Hill. Years later, most of the bodies in that graveyard were exhumed and reburied in Belvedere and Mount Carmel cemeteries.

Catherine Snow wasn't long in the ground before rumours began to circulate throughout St. John's that her ghost had been seen in the area where she had been hanged. The stories were reported in the local newspapers. Soon, people came forward to say that they had seen her ghost in the Catholic cemetery.

Years passed, and the tragedy of Catherine Snow was all but forgotten. Then, in the 1950s, a pair of cleaning women who worked in the courthouse claimed that they had seen the ghost of a woman wandering through it at night. Old timers who knew of Catherine's story were sure that the apparition the women had seen was that of Catherine Snow. Could it be that Catherine's spirit could not rest because the law had in fact hanged an innocent woman?

The Duelist's Ghost

For hundreds of years, right up into the nineteenth century, any military officer or upper-class civilian who considered himself a gentleman subscribed to a code that required him to demand satisfaction on the field of honour should he ever be publicly insulted. Even after dueling was outlawed throughout the British Empire, men with scores to settle challenged each other to ritualized combat with swords or pistols. The would-be duelists' seconds, or honorary representatives, would often manage to negotiate a satisfactory compromise before any actual violence occurred. Failing such a peaceful resolution, the duelists and their seconds would meet at a prearranged location — out of sight of the law — to cross swords or exchange shots at twenty paces. A duel with swords usually ended with the first nick to draw blood. In pistol duels, the matter was often considered honourably settled after one exchange of shots, even if both shooters missed. Duels did not always end in death; but very often they did. One such fatal duel gave rise to the legend of a famous St. John's ghost.

On a snowy evening in late March 1826, the officers of Fort Townshend were in their quarters drinking rum toddies and passing the time at cards. It's uncertain what game they were playing, but the officers were definitely gambling. Two of the players were Captain Mark Rudkin of the British army, and twenty-seven-year-old Ensign John Philpot of the Royal Veteran Company. Apparently, these two men were more than just opponents in a card game; they were also rivals for the affections of a pretty Irish girl who lived near Quidi Vidi. Philpot had allegedly been goaded into insulting Rudkin earlier at a social function, but had apologized.

Philpot was losing money in the game. As the evening wore on and his losses increased, he drank too much and became quarrelsome. Other players folded their hands and left the table, until only Captain Rudkin and Ensign Philpot remained.

It was the last hand of the game: a showdown, with Rudkin dealing. The pot on the table totalled two pounds, eight shillings, and sixpence, which was a considerable sum at that time. Philpot desperately wanted to win it and recoup at least some of his losses. But Rudkin dealt himself the winning hand.

Rudkin started to pull in his winnings, but Philpot accused him of cheating and seized the money. Not one to be intimidated by some whelp of an ensign, Captain Rudkin forcibly took the money back and headed for the door. Drunk and enraged, Philpot pursued Rudkin. He threw a drink in the captain's face and, to the astonishment of all present, kicked him on the backside. Rudkin had been insulted three times in the presence of his fellow officers; he challenged Philpot to a duel.

The following morning, March 30, the antagonists met on a field near Brine's Tavern at Robinson's Hill, which was about a mile outside of town. Philpot's second was Captain George Farquhar Morice, commander of HMS *Grasshopper*. He tried to talk the young man out of proceeding with the fight. But Philpot was still angry and insisted that Rudkin had been cheating.

Rudkin's second was Dr. James Coulter Strachan, an army surgeon. Rudkin was a twenty-two-year veteran of the British army who had fought in several campaigns and been wounded in battle. He had cooled down, following his outrage of the night before, and offered to call off the duel. But Philpot would have none of it.

The two men were given loaded pistols and took up their firing positions. Rudkin cleverly placed himself so that the rising sun was at his back, leaving Philpot to squint into the morning glare. Dr. Strachan gave the signal and both men fired. Philpot's bullet nicked Rudkin's collar; Rudkin, a crack shot, fired his gun into the air. With gunsmoke floating in the air, and neither duelist hurt, Rudkin and the seconds were willing to let the matter rest. Philpot demanded a second exchange.

The guns were reloaded, and this time Morice gave the signal. According to different versions of the story, either Rudkin or Philpot leapt into the air as he fired. Such an action might have made a man a more difficult target for his opponent to hit, but it would have thrown off his own aim. If anyone actually jumped, it was likely Philpot, and it would have been because Rudkin's bullet struck him in the chest, just above the heart, while his own shot went wild. The young ensign fell dead, a victim of his own foolishness and an archaic code of honour. He was buried in the Anglican churchyard, ironically, on April Fool's day.

News of the fatal duel spread through St. John's, and Captain Rudkin and the seconds were arrested. Rudkin was charged with murder, and the seconds with being accessories. Public sympathy was initially on the side of the slain ensign, but it eventually shifted in favour of the captain. At the trial on April 17, the jury found Rudkin and the seconds not guilty. A crowd of friends and supporters carried them on their shoulders from the courthouse to the fort on Garrison Hill.

Not long after the trial, stories began to circulate that a restless spirit had been seen near the dueling grounds. It was said that when Captain Rudkin was on his way to the fatal encounter, his horse had become skittish, almost as though it sensed something bad was about to occur. After the duel, other horses also shied away from the place.

People who claimed to have seen the ghost said it wore a military uniform and had a bloodstain on the breast. Years later the area in which the ghost had been sighted became popular with courting couples. Perhaps the idea of a ghost lurking nearby was a good excuse for a young lady to huddle close to her young man.

During the construction of St. John's Anglican Cathedral, a grave that was possibly that of Ensign Philpot was exhumed. Ghostly lore suggests that the spirits of the departed do not rest well when their earthly remains are disturbed. In the urban developments that have spread over the ground where Ensign John Philpot took an unwise stand on the field of honour, perhaps his spirit still wanders, lamenting having been cheated once more, this time out of his final resting place.

The Haunted Hotel Room

Movies like Alfred Hitchcock's thriller *Psycho*, and novels such as *The Shining* by Stephen King are modern — and masterful — variations on a very old suspicion held by nervous travellers: smiling innkeepers might not be as hospitable as they appear; and places of lodging, however comfortable, do not necessarily guarantee a safe night's sleep. Traveller's lore is full of stories about murders that are committed in hotel and motel rooms, and of unwary guests who find themselves sharing accommodations with a lingering spirit. St. John's has not, thankfully, had the equivalent of Norman Bates sitting at a hotel registration desk. But it has had a hotel haunting that would impress even Stephen King.

Foran's Hotel on Water St. in St. John's stood on the site now occupied by the Post Office. It was one of many lodging businesses catering to travellers in the busy seaport. One night, sometime early in the twentieth century, the guests were awakened by a loud knocking. Two men traced the racket to an upstairs room. As soon as they entered, the knocking stopped. The men searched the room, but couldn't find the source of the noise.

This became a nightly occurrence. Guests would awake to loud knocking, but as soon as someone entered that room, the noise stopped. Business began to suffer, because people were afraid that the hotel was haunted. After a few months the knocking stopped, and the guests came back. But nobody would stay in that room.

Water Street, St. John's, circa 1880. St. John's is North America's oldest city, and according to local paranormal experts, also its most haunted.

One day a stranger who was unfamiliar with the story of the strange room came to Foran's Hotel. Every room in the hotel was occupied except the one from which the knocking had come. The manager didn't want to send the stranger to another hotel and, since the room had been quiet for a long time, decided it would be okay to give the room to the man. The staff found it amusing to finally have a guest in that room.

At midnight everyone in the hotel was awoken by a thunderous knocking. As guests stood in the corridor wondering what was happening, the manager went to the stranger's room and opened the door. The knocking immediately stopped. When the manager entered the room, he saw the stranger lying on the floor, dead! He had a look of terror on his face. When an undertaker came to remove the body, the knocking commenced again, but lasted for only a minute. The stranger, who was never identified, was buried in the cemetery on Waterford Bridge Road. The exact location of the grave was eventually lost.

After the mysterious death of the stranger the knocking stopped. Nonetheless, the hotel's management closed the room to the public. Foran's Hotel was eventually torn down, and the General Post Office was built on the site. That structure in turn was replaced in the 1960s by a modern office building that is used by Canada Post. Before long, postal workers began to report strange knocking noises in one of the upper rooms. If the cause of the knocking is the same as that which disturbed the guests in Foran's Hotel, then this location is one of the oldest continuously haunted sites in St. John's.

The Missing Gravestone

Whether we call it a tombstone, gravestone, monument, or simply a marker, it is a final, and hopefully lasting, signal to the world that the person lying beneath it once walked the earth. It might be a simple, unadorned slab of stone, or it could be a large, elaborate work of art worthy of a Renaissance sculptor. The inscription below the person's name is usually their birth and death dates, but there could also be a moving epitaph. There might even be, as in Shakespeare's case, a curse on the stone. But whether grave markers are humble or ostentatious, it is evident from the numerous ghost stories associated with them that if they are violated, the spirits of the departed do not rest in peace.

Alice Janes was a colourful figure in nineteenth-century St. John's. A frequent patron at the racetrack, she was usually seen wearing an Irish-knit shawl and holding a jug of brew. In fact, Alice died at the racetrack of a sudden heart attack. Almost everyone in town attended her funeral. She was buried in the old cemetery adjacent to the Anglican Cathedral.

A year later, on the anniversary of Alice's death, a young couple was strolling through Flower Hill field near racetrack. It was dusk, and the woman suddenly noticed a sharp chill. She asked her companion to take her home. As they neared the edge of the field, they saw something that made them turn and run.

At first they thought they saw an old woman sitting on a rock, holding a jug in her hand. But as they drew near, the figure stood up straight and looked right at them. It was a hag, with fiery red eyes, and white hair that stood out like the whisks on a broom: the young couple recognized the apparition as Alice Janes.

When the story of the ghost spread around town, Alice's friends went to the cemetery to pray at her grave. They immediately saw that the gravestone was missing. They searched all through the cemetery, but could not find it.

For the next ten years, Alice Janes's ghost could be seen in the same place on the anniversary of her death. Until one day while clearing out an isolated corner of the cemetery, the caretaker found the missing gravestone and respectfully returned it to its proper location. After that, Alice Janes' ghost was never seen again.

The Cry of the Banshee

In Celtic lore, a banshee is a death-omen spirit. It was often the ghost of a woman who had died in childbirth, and was cursed to roam the earth until the time of her naturally destined death. A banshee would attach itself to a family, giving warnings of impending death. The banshee was usually heard, but not seen. Her warning of an approaching death came in the form of mournful singing or loud wailing. The cry was said to be so sorrowful that it was unmistakably a harbinger of doom. On the rare occasions that a banshee was seen, it appeared as a woman — usually beautiful, but sometimes a hag — with fiery eyes, dressed in white or red. It might also appear as a figure flying in the moonlight. The Celtic people of the British Isles carried the legend of the banshee with them to Newfoundland.

William Welsh was a successful and well-respected businessman in St. John's at the end of the eighteenth century. He owned a public house and banquet hall on the west side of Hill O'Chips. Welsh was descended from the chiefs of Barony, Ireland, where the first Welsh had been a warrior chief. There was a tradition in the family that a banshee's cry would always foretell a death or misfortune. William dismissed this as superstitious nonsense, even though his wife and family firmly believed it.

One night, Mrs. Welsh suddenly became distraught. She told her husband that she had heard the cry of a banshee. "It was like a weirdly wailing and sobbing keen, coming nearer and nearer each moment until it reached the window," she said. "Then with a wild shriek it died away with unearthly sobbing. Anyone hearing it would never forget it."

A banshee wrings her hands in despair in this old Scottish illustration. The cry of a banshee was heard before the death of William Welsh of St. John's.

William had heard nothing, and thought his wife was imagining things. The next day, however, their youngest son Felix cut himself badly with an axe while chopping firewood and almost bled to death. William still refused to believe in the banshee.

Several years later, Welsh was celebrating his sixtieth birthday. He was sitting at the head of the table in his banquet hall, enjoying a meal with some of St. John's most prominent citizens, including a colonel named Skinner from the British garrison. Suddenly the door flew open and William's eldest son, Michael, burst into the room. The young man was ashen faced, and oblivious to everyone except his father. Before the stunned dinner guests he said to William, "We all heard the cry tonight! Are you all right?"

Surprised by the sudden intrusion, William said, "Of course I am. Why wouldn't I be? I'm as healthy as an ox."

Satisfied that his father was all right, Michael left. Colonel Skinner asked Welsh what Michael had meant by "the cry." William told his guests the legend of the Welsh family and the cry of the banshee. He said it was all childish superstition, and most of the diners agreed. Colonel Skinner, however, wasn't so sure about that.

After all the guests had left, Welsh admonished his family for believing in a silly superstition. "No one should concern himself about me," he said. "I never felt better in my life."

The following morning at breakfast, with no warning whatsoever, William Welsh dropped dead!

Colonel Skinner was stunned when he heard the news. "I can't believe it," he said. "He was so healthy!" But recalling the story Welsh had told him, he added, "There was something in the banshee's cry after all."

Cold Fire

People have always been in awe of fire: it is a warm and useful tool, to be respected and feared. It's no small wonder that fire has many supernatural connotations, from the punishments of hell to the mysterious blazes that sometimes accompany poltergeist activity. One of the strangest fiery phenomenon, though, is that of fire that burns without burning.

Willicott's Lane is in one of the oldest parts of St. John's. In the early nineteenth century it was part of a crowded slum district that featured shoddy houses and smelly open-ditch sewers. This unsightly neighbourhood was completely gutted by fire in 1855. It was rebuilt only to be destroyed again in the Great Fire of St. John's in 1892. That this section of the city was twice devoured by flames may be the reason that a building there is haunted by cold fire.

One of the houses that was built after the Great Fire backed onto Willicott's Lane. For many years its sole occupant was an old woman. She died in the house sometime in the mid-twentieth century, and her house remained empty for a while following her death.

Or did it?

From time to time, passersby would notice a flickering light in a second storey window — the kind of light produced by a blazing fireplace. Concerned about a fire in what was supposed to be a vacant house, they would go in to investigate. While there was never anyone in the house, each inquisitive passerby would find a fire burning in the fireplace of a second storey bedroom. After a minute, the flames would disappear right before their eyes, as though the fire had never been there. When the bewildered witnesses touched the bricks, they were cold. This strange event allegedly continued to occur periodically even after new owners took possession of the house.

The phenomenon took a different turn in the 1980s, when a male tenant was renting the house. He was in bed on the same floor as the room with the mysterious fire when his bedroom door suddenly flew open. He could see into the hall, and was startled by the flicker of firelight dancing on the walls.

Nobody else was in the house, so there was no reason for fire to be burning in any of the fireplaces. The man got out of bed to investigate, and found nothing: the strange lights had vanished.

Perplexed, the man went back to bed. His head had barely touched the pillow, when his door swept open again! Firelight once more reflected off the walls of the hallway. The man looked in the other bedroom, but found no fire. The bricks and the iron grate in the fireplace were cold to the touch.

To the man's exasperation, this happened a *third* time! Was he imagining things? Was this a waking dream? Were the flickers he had seen just reflections of car lights from the street?

If so, what caused his door to open on its own three times? And what was the explanation for the phantom flames earlier witnesses had seen in the fireplace? Was this an extraordinary form of residual haunting, left over from one of the devastating conflagrations? The Cold Fire case remains an intriguing St. John's mystery.

A Nightmare on Gower Street

In the nineteenth century and the first half of the twentieth century, it was not uncommon to see haunted house stories reported in the papers as news items. People took their stories of strange experiences to the press, hoping they would be taken seriously. One such story tells the tale of a nightmarish haunting that was no laughing matter.

In 1907 a Newfoundland couple who had been living in the United States returned to St. John's to visit for a few months. They rented a house on Gower Street, and paid for their three month stay in advance. They'd have been better off paying by the week: on the very first night, something happened that made them flee the house in terror.

According to a report in the St. John's *Evening Telegram*, "... the woman had been startled in the night by a series of blood-curdling screeches. Horrified she sat up in bed and saw a woman who had been known to her, but had died several years before in the same room."

As if one ghost was not enough, this house was haunted by *two*. "The apparition was dragging another woman, also known to be dead, by the hair of her head. The woman being dragged was screaming."

The woman who witnessed this unnerving scene was so frightened, she fell into a faint. She was revived at daybreak, upon which she and her husband immediately packed up their belongings and left the house, swearing that they would never set foot in it again. It was, as it turned out, a costly fright they'd had: the landlord refused to refund their rent money.

Case Files: St. John's

The Knights of Columbus Fire: Mother Knew

Call it women's intuition or mother's instinct. There have been many recorded instances of mothers knowing that one of their children is in great danger, even though that child is far away and there is no possible way the mother could have known the situation. Are these women psychic? Perhaps. Or it could be that maternal love has a power that goes beyond intellectual comprehension. An example of this psychic power occurred during one of the greatest tragedies in the history of St. John's.

The Knights of Columbus auditorium on Harvey Street was built in 1941. It was meant to be a home away from home for Canadian and American servicemen and members of the Newfoundland militia during the dark days of the Second World War. The ground floor had a grand hall for dances and other events, a restaurant, and a games room. The second floor served as a hostel where servicemen on leave could spend the night.

The building was constructed almost entirely of wood, and there were serious flaws in its design as far as fire regulations were concerned. All of its doors, including the ones on the only two emergency exits, opened inward, which meant they would be impossible to open if a crowd of panic-stricken people were in a rush to get out. There was no unobstructed route from the main hall to the exit. There was no emergency lighting system. Wartime regulations demanded that windows be blacked out at night, but instead of blinds or heavy curtains,

The Rooms Provincial Archives of Newfoundland and Labrador.

The Knights of Columbus Fire in St. John's. Miles away, in St. Mary's Bay, Elizabeth Ryan somehow knew that her sons were in danger.

the hall's windows were covered with sheets of plywood that were nailed in place. The Knights of Columbus building was essentially a firetrap. To add to the built-in hazards, on the night of December 12, 1942, the main hall was decked out with highly flammable Christmas decorations.

A dance was being held that night, and the place was packed with over four hundred people. Most of the guests were servicemen, but many local girls were there to enjoy an evening of dancing and entertainment. Providing the music was William Patrick "Uncle Tim" Duggan and his Barn Dance troupe, which included three of his sons. The band's performance was being broadcast by radio from the auditorium's stage.

Among the people enjoying the festivities were Gabriel and Laurence Ryan from St. Mary's Bay. In their home town, more than a hundred miles away, their mother Elizabeth had her radio tuned to the broadcast. As she listened, the radio suddenly went dead. Elizabeth thought that technical problems were the cause, so she switched the radio off and began to prepare for bed. It was after 11:00 p.m., and the Knights of Columbus Auditorium had become a raging inferno.

A Canadian soldier named Eddie Adams was on stage singing a cowboy song called "The Midnight Trail" when the main hall was suddenly engulfed in flames, smoke, and blisteringly hot gas. Terrified people rushed for the doors, but couldn't open them. Many were asphyxiated right where they stood. Men in flaming pajamas jumped from second floor windows. The lights went out, leaving parts of the building in smoke-choked darkness. And a fuse box blew, rendering the radio equipment mute. In those first terrible moments, nobody outside the Knights of Columbus Auditorium knew that people were being roasted alive.

But in St. Mary's Bay, Elizabeth Ryan suddenly felt that something was terribly wrong. She was walking through the house, when she felt something brush against her leg. At first she thought it was the family's cat, but when she looked for the pet, it was nowhere to be seen. Elizabeth was certain, though, that *something* had touched her!

Suddenly, Elizabeth was overcome with an inexplicable feeling of dread. Something told her that her sons were in mortal danger. "I knelt on my knees and I prayed. I prayed the whole night," Elizabeth said later.

Elizabeth Ryan and other members of her family continued to worry and pray for another day and a half, not knowing for certain what had happened. News of the disaster gradually spread to Newfoundland's rural communities. The fire had killed 99 people, including Uncle Tim's son Gus. Many of the survivors were badly burned. Elizabeth finally received a telegram informing her that Gabriel and Laurence were alive and well.

There was strong evidence that the fire had been started by an arsonist, quite possibly a Nazi agent. But this was never proven and no suspects were ever arrested. Thus, two mysteries were left with the ashes of the Knights of Columbus Auditorium. Who started the fire, and how did Elizabeth Ryan know, without being told, that her sons' lives were in danger?

The Ghost Next Door

Most people who have had a paranormal experience and have tried to talk about it with family or friends find that their listeners either accept the story as true, or they dismiss it as a fabrication. They might even suggest that the person telling the story is slightly crazy. The following story came to me by email from Sharon in Toronto.

✝

I'm from Toronto, but for two years my husband and I lived in St. John's, Newfoundland, due to my husband's work. I won't say exactly where this "ghost story" happened, because the people who lived next door to us didn't believe me when I told them what I saw. I'll just say it was on a residential street in St. John's.

We lived in a two-storey house, and from the window of the main bedroom you could see into our backyard and the next-door neighbours' backyards. I liked looking out the window with the lights turned off for a little while every night, because on a clear night you could see so many stars. It was better than reading a book to relax you. In one of the houses next to us there was a family with a grandfather I'll call Joe. When the weather was nice, Joe liked to sit under a big tree in the backyard. I think it was his favourite place. They had a picnic table back there, and Joe would sit at it, reading his newspaper and smoking his pipe. He always wore one of those cloth caps that my husband called a Depression hat, because men wore them in the thirties.

This family used to call us Mainlanders as a little joke, but they were always friendly and we got to know them pretty good. After we were there for about a year and a half, old Joe died. It was in July. That afternoon I saw him sitting in his backyard with his pipe, his newspaper, and a cup of tea: that night he just passed away in his sleep. My husband and I were stunned when we heard, because you wouldn't have thought there was anything wrong with the dear old man. I helped out with the food for the wake, and we went to the funeral.

One night about a week later, I was looking out my window when I thought I saw something move in the neighbours' backyard. It was dark, but there was enough moonlight that you could see the picnic table. There was a man sitting at it.

At first I thought it was our neighbour, Joe's son. I wondered what he was doing out there alone in the dark. Then I thought he must be grieving over his father, and I thought I shouldn't be watching him at such a private time, and I'd better get my face out of the window. But then

I saw him move again, and I think it was the same movement that caught my eye in the first place. He moved his arm like he was turning the page of a newspaper, except there was no newspaper.

Suddenly I felt goosebumps all over me. It wasn't the son. It was *Joe*! I blinked and looked again, and sure enough it *was* Joe. He didn't look shadowy or misty, the way you sometimes read about ghosts. He looked like a solid man. He was even wearing his old cap. All that was missing was his pipe.

My husband was downstairs. I didn't want to call to him, because I had the feeling that if I did, Joe or his ghost or whatever it was would hear and look up at me, and I think I would have died on the spot if he looked at me. I went downstairs and asked my husband to come back up with me. It was late, so he turned off the TV and came up. While he was getting ready for bed, I peeked out the window. If Joe was still there I was going to tell my husband to come and look. But there was nothing there. I didn't even tell my husband about it.

Over the next few nights I was half-afraid to look out my window, and half-needing to see if something would be there. I peeked out a few times, but everything was normal. I started to think I must have imagined it, and I was glad that I didn't say anything to anyone because they would have thought I was crazy.

Then it happened again, and this time my husband saw it, too. It was a couple of weeks after the first time. We were both in bed, and the curtains were still open. My husband got up to close them. Then he said, "Who's that down there?"

I got up and looked out the window with him. There was the same thing I saw before. An old man wearing an old fashioned cap, and moving his arms like he was turning pages of a newspaper. He looked as solid as the tree. After almost a minute my husband said in sort of a whisper, "Holy Jesus! That looks like Joe!"

I whispered that we better get away from the window before he sees us. I backed away, but my husband kept looking. I sort of hissed at him, telling him to come on. Then he said, "He's gone. There's nobody there now."

I told him to make sure he closed the curtains all the way. I liked old Joe, but I didn't like the idea of his ghost floating up and looking in our window.

We went to bed, but it was a long time before we got to sleep. I told him that I had already seen it once before. Neither of us had ever believed in ghosts. We heard stories, the same as everybody does, and we even heard about some old buildings in St. John's that were supposed to be haunted. But we never really believed any of it. We might not have believed what we saw that night, if it wasn't that we both saw it.

I said that maybe we should tell them — our neighbours. Maybe they saw it too, and might be wondering if they were going crazy or something. My husband said no, we should just keep quiet. He said they were in grief, and they didn't need outsiders poking their noses in with crazy stories. But I thought they should know. We weren't the only ones with a window that looked into that backyard. Maybe other neighbours saw it and were talking about it right at that moment. If that was the case, then Joe's family was going to hear some kind of gossip sooner or later. We were in St. John's long enough to know that gossip got around faster than anything. So my husband said okay, we'll talk to them.

The next day after supper, we asked them, Joe's son and his wife, to come over for a cup of tea. We were sitting at the kitchen table, having some tea and smokes, and just chatting. Then my husband brought it up. He was a bit awkward about it, but he asked them if anyone was in their backyard late the night before, sitting at the picnic table.

They looked at each other and then said no. Then my husband said, "Well, last night we saw somebody, and it looked like your father."

We told them what we saw, and what I saw that other time. Then Joe's son said we must have been mistaken. He said that his father was in heaven. Whatever we thought we saw, it was not Joe. He asked us if we told anyone else about this, and we said no. He said he would be grateful if we did not say another word about it to anybody, including them. He was nice, but you could tell he meant it.

It was about six months after that time that my husband got transferred back to Toronto. We didn't see the ghost again, but I must admit that I closed all the curtains tight every night and I felt too spooked to look at the stars. I did have a couple of bad dreams about seeing the ghost's face looking in the window. I don't know if any of the other neighbours ever saw anything.

Q & A with Gene Browne

Name of Organization: NPI — Newfoundland Paranormal Investigation
  group
Date Founded: September 2008
Website: *sites.google.com/site/nlparanormalinvestigation/*
Mission: This group was created to assist those in need of help with
  paranormal activity occurring within their daily lives. This group was
  also created to make people aware that there are others who are willing
  to listen to their stories and claims without the fear of being judged.
Founder and Lead Investigator: Mike Barnes and Gene Browne.
Description of Organization (Who we are): Mike Barnes, Gene Browne,
  Nicole Squires, Patrina Barnes, and Diana Leadbeater.
Favourite Newfoundland & Labrador Haunt: The whole city of St. John's.

Q: How long have you been investigating the paranormal?
A: Personally, I have been interested in it all my life since I can
    remember. As a group we're fairly new, so we haven't had much time
    to have many cases. I've been researching for about ten years now.

Q: When did your own interest
    begin?
A: When I was five years old.
    We lived in one of the oldest
    houses in my community,
    which ended up being torn
    down and was apparently
    built on three graves.
    The headstones are still
    available for viewing in my
    community heritage house.

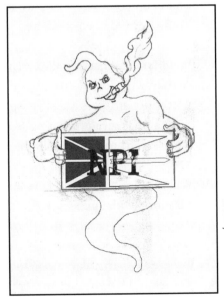

Logo of the Newfoundland Paranormal Investigators.

Q: What is your community heritage house?

A: The O'Reilly Heritage House. It's one of the oldest in the community, and it serves as our little museum.

Q: How did that interest progress?

A: The houses I lived in after that continued to be haunted.

Q: Can you give some examples of what was happening in those houses?

A: We would be on the main floor of one house, and we'd hear a basketball bouncing in the room upstairs, and computer chairs sliding around the hardwood floors. We'd always check it out, and the ball would be still in the closet and the chair would be into the desk. Voices. Footsteps. One house we lived in, we'd hear music coming from different rooms, and when we entered, it'd just stop. The same house, you could hear the front door opening and people walking across the floors, only for no one to be there. They were prominent steps, too; not just other sounds we assumed were steps. We had a toilet paper rack and a towel rack ripped out of the wall in another house. In the same place, our clothes would be thrown all over the basement out of the dryer. We've had a lot of experiences in a lot of different areas. This is one haunted city; and if not haunted, it has some kind of energy here.

Q: Would you say that you take a skeptical approach to a new investigation?

A: Certainly. A lot of "hauntings" can be easily explained through conventional issues such as plumbing, electrical, old housing, etc. You can't believe everything is a ghost. When common sense and science don't explain it, it's something else.

Q: What are some of the explanations you've found to what appear to be paranormal phenomena?

A: Plumbing, electrical, settling houses, faulty devices.

Q: Is there any particular reason that you haven't worked with psychics?

A: Not really. I haven't met any, or found the need to go find one.

Q: What equipment do you use to investigate?

A: Digital recorders, video cameras, infrared cameras, and scrying crystals.

Q: What are scrying crystals?

A: Scrying — also called crystal gazing, crystal seeing, seeing, or peeping — is a magic practice that involves seeing things psychically in a medium, usually for purposes of obtaining spiritual visions, and more rarely for purposes of divination or fortune telling. The media used are most commonly reflective, translucent, or luminescent substances such as crystals, stones, glass, mirrors, fire, or smoke. Scrying has been used in many cultures as a means of divining the past, present, or future. Depending on the culture or practice, the visions that come when one stares into the medium are thought to come from God, spirits, the psychic mind, the devil, or the subconscious. But you can also use one by letting it hang and trying to get entities to interact with it; using their energy to move it, etc.

Q: Are there certain criteria that must be met before you agree to an investigation? What conditions must a potential client meet to convince you to take a case?

A: Well it has to be a more than once occurrence. You have to reside in Newfoundland. Children being tormented is certainly an eye opener.

Q: Children being tormented. Can you describe an instance of that?

A: Well, I can give you a personal experience. When I was a kid, five years old, we lived next to the heritage house in our community. We were always hearing things and having various experiences. One night I woke up to a man in my window with this old hat on; the hat looked really old, like 1600s, and he had a huge knife in his hand. I screamed, like you would, and Mom and Dad came in. They said it was just a dream. But to today I know that it wasn't. The house was eventually torn down, and under it were three graves of Basque fishermen, from the 1600s. Pretty crazy! Other instances would be something keeping children awake during the night, interacting with them because they're so impressionable. There are numerous accounts of such things around the web.

Q: Do your clients ask for evidence, or do they want you to disprove a paranormal existence in their home or business to put them at ease?
A: Both.

Q: Is your primary mission to find answers regarding the existence of ghosts, or to help people who are living with them?
A: Our primary mission is to find answers, period; whether it's regarding the existence of ghosts, non-existence or whatever it may be. We share our opinions and thoughts with the client regarding living with what's going on.

Q: Are the ghost-hunting programs on TV very accurate?
A: I like *Ghost Hunters* due to the equipment they use. Because they're on TV they're spiced up a little to get those extra ratings, but out of them all I think that they're fairly accurate. I've gotten some similar findings on some of my personal investigations, so I think they are.

Q: Do you have a favourite case?
A: They're all exciting. But being a new team, we don't have many to go on.

Q: What do you see in the future for your organization?
A: I see big things. As you see more skeptics popping up, you see more believers and people who are opening their minds to such things as the possibility of ghosts and other entities in their presence, so I think once we get that big case, we'll be off to the races, as they say.

Q: How do you decide who you will allow to go on an investigation with you?
A: Someone has to be a very rational person, confident in themselves and the rest of the team, someone who is very knowledgeable in the field, and someone who doesn't scare easily.

Q: Do you think a paranormal investigation could result in a scientific breakthrough?

A: One hundred percent for sure. It's only a matter of time before those few pieces of irrefutable evidence are put forward and will allow us to make progress in the field.

Q: Have you ever felt you were in danger during an investigation?

A: No.

Q: Do you learn everything you can about a location before you actually go there?

A: It certainly helps.

Q: In what ways?

A: Well, if you know a place has had some problems with electrical, plumbing, other everyday things, a lot of times stories and claims can be debunked through some investigation of such things. Knowing certain history can help you figure out as well what could be haunting a place, if it is haunted. Some places which are built near quartz and limestone are prone to hauntings because the quartz stores energy so well. So if there was once a lot of energy present, chances are it's being replayed over time. A little pre-knowledge can help you big time on any given investigation.

Q: What about cases where you don't find anything?

A: Sometimes it's possible that you find nothing, no matter how much investigating you do. These places have the possibility of not being haunted, or [are] just quiet that night.

Q: What sort of evidence do you look for?

A: Disembodied voices, full body apparitions, unexplained sounds, communication of any kind.

Q: What type of person is best suited for this work?

A: Anyone interested in helping people who are interested in the paranormal, and those who love it.

Q: What can bring an entity, friendly or unfriendly, into a building?
A: Death, trauma, Ouija board, spirit boards, magic.

Q: What is a spirit board? What sort of "magic" can bring an entity into a building?
A: A spirit board is just another name for a Ouija board. Magic, in the paranormal sense is sometimes known as sorcery. It is the practice of the manipulation of consciousness and/or the use of auto-suggestion to achieve a desired result. When you use magic, you're using unseen forces in the universe that are not really well understood. Opening doors and windows to things you are not well-educated on, and therefore have not taken the proper precautions, can invite something in. It can be good or bad. When using such arts, you have to be knowledgeable and well-prepared.

Q: Are Ouija boards dangerous?
A: If the belief is strong enough, and it's used inappropriately.

Q: Are people's attitudes regarding the paranormal changing?
A: I think so. More and more people believe in something ... out the ordinary ... or the paranormal.

Gene Browne's Haunted House

This story happened in the fall of 2004 in St. John's, Newfoundland, while I was attending Memorial University. This was my second year in St. John's and I was pretty much unfamiliar with the whole city, and never thought much of any ghosts here — and after being burned down three times, it certainly has its history. My roommates and I spent most of the summer looking for a nice house to rent, and with two weeks left at the end of August we found one. The house was awesome and very comfortable. There were two and a half bedrooms and the bathroom upstairs, and a living room, dining room, and kitchen were downstairs. My room was the dining room on the main floor because the half-bedroom just wasn't big enough.

The first few nights staying there were fairly interesting. We spent pretty much the whole time searching for the furnace temperature control as our "furnace" wouldn't stop turning on, and the weather was warm enough that it shouldn't have been happening. We never found it, and shortly discovered we had no furnace in our basement, just a hot water boiler: all the heat was electric. So for the duration of our time there we never really found out what it was that had been heating up the house, and we looked. That was pretty much the start of maybe the weirdest and most memorable seven weeks of my life. I moved out after seven weeks: it actually got to be too much even for a paranormal junkie like me. I always remember these stories; most of them happened with groups of people around, which adds to the validity of them — or the insanity of the group.

During the first few weeks of living there, my roommate, who I'll call Stef, was having dreams of a little girl who lived in the attic, wore a yellow dress, and was always whistling the same song. She told us about it but it never really meant anything or had any impact, until after three or four weeks of living there. We'd been having a bunch of strange occurrences: lights on and off, footsteps, doors opening and closing, voices, pretty much everything associated with a usual haunting. Myself, being super interested in the whole field and being someone who pretty much lived with ghosts all my life, I was intrigued and not-so-scared as it wasn't hurting anyone, just toying with us. Even though I was aware that similar things happen with hauntings, we didn't really think ghost as much as we did, you know, an old house settling and creaking. As for the voices, we attributed them to TVs being on in other rooms. We didn't jump at the possibility of it being ghosts right away.

After about three or four weeks there it was happening more and more. Our friends who were staying over were getting really freaked out.

It even came to a point where we were setting up beds in my room so they didn't have to stay in the living room alone because the lights were flicking on and off while they were lying there — not to mention it was on a broken dimmer that could only be rotated to be turned off, as the push function was broken. So for a light to flick on and off very rapidly meant the dial was being turned at incredible speeds to give the same effect. We got the wiring checked out by the landlords just to make sure everything was okay and we weren't in risk of a fire, and it was all fine.

One night while myself and four of my friends were chilling out and eating some pizza, the guys were talking about how "busy" the house was and wanted to do a Ouija Board. Being an enthusiast I'd heard of such things, but had never done one up until this point. It took some convincing but I eventually gave in.

We used an old pizza box because I had read that a homemade board would be better than a store bought one, and being late in the evening and not having much to work with, this is what was used. We set up the board, got some candles, put a ring of salt around us for protection, and began using it. For the first little bit it was moving slow, but about thirty minutes or more in, the planchette was having no trouble moving. Ouija Boards are full of speculation that it's just people pushing it around, consciously or subconsciously. But this night changed my mind. It got to the point where we were having fun talking to some "spirits" that claimed to be living in the house with us: a little boy who lived in the basement and a little girl who claimed to live in the attic. Then it started to get a little freaky, because everyone had known the story of the whistling girl Stef had seen. And you know what? When we were talking to her, we asked her to prove it was her. We heard whistling from the top of the stairs, and all five of us heard it. We continued using the board, but one of my friends was becoming skeptical because it was *too real* and working too well. So he starting saying, you know if you're real, show us some signs, which is a bad idea. You shouldn't invite anything into your house, whether you believe in it or not.

He kept asking, and that's when it picked up. My other roommate was the drummer in my band. All his drums were packed up neatly on the back porch in their cases. Suddenly, it sounded like something was hitting them as you could hear them resonate. We could see them, so we knew it was them, but we didn't know what was causing the noise. We attributed it to a coincidence, and said it might have been a mouse. We kept going and my friend kept asking for a sign. Eventually it got to the point where the dishes were rattling in the cupboards and food was sliding around inside them. It was starting to get out of hand, and he quickly turned into a believer.

We continued to have more experiences, and the planchette — we were using an old egg cup that night — was starting to move really fast, at times with no hands on it, which is why what the board was made of was an important point. With the heat ripple from the pizza in the middle of the board, fast movements would have just tipped the cup over, or at least you wouldn't get a smooth slide at a fast speed. It was pretty crazy.

So after various conversations with multiple entities that "lived" in the house and came through the board, we decided to give up and call it a night. We cleaned up the whole area and just went to the living room to relax after some pretty crazy experiences. We were all sitting on the couches when the guy who was asking for signs jumped up off the couch and freaked out. Something had grabbed his leg and he said it wasn't cool for us to be messing with him. He figured it was our other friend who was sitting next to him, but I saw that it wasn't, because I was looking in both their directions. His eyes began to water and he said that he didn't really believe it, but it's just too much for him right now. So he convinced us all to leave. We stayed at a friend's house until seven a.m. when it became light again.

After the Ouija Board night, the happenings in the house remained constant, if not more so now. This all led to the event that made me move out. One weekend my two roommates had left the house to go back to our hometown to visit their parents, leaving me alone in the house for the weekend. I didn't mind at all. So I got up midday Friday and made my way out of my room to the kitchen to get a glass of water. Normally, in a house with three university students, a kitchen full of dirty dishes isn't out of the ordinary. But today was different. I never paid attention to them, got my drink, and went back to my room. Two hours or more later, I came back out of my room and was going to tidy up the whole house, starting with the kitchen. But when I got there, there were *no dirty dishes* in the kitchen. My brain kind of hurt, and I was convincing myself that earlier I had been dreaming that I gotten up and got some water, and that the whole thing never really happened. It's the only thing you *can* tell yourself in a situation like that. So from there I went with the thought that I dreamt that I had gotten up for water, and the roommates had cleaned up before they left. So I just went back to my room to relax and clear my mind after that.

But two hours later I went back and the dishes were everywhere again! I honestly called my parents and told them I thought I had a mental problem. I couldn't process the situation, and I don't know how anyone else could either. You walk into a room; there's dirty dishes. Then there's none two hours later; then they're back. And you're home alone! It's a tough pill to swallow. I called up a friend and asked if I could stay over the weekend. It ended up being my last weekend in the house: I didn't want to stick around and see where it was all going. My roommates lived there for a few months longer than me and eventually moved out as well. That house was pretty freaky.

Oft Told Tales: Literature and Folklore

The Oral Tradition

The oral tradition — the passing of stories by word of mouth from one generation to the next — has its oldest roots in Canada among the various peoples of the First Nations. However, because the Native inhabitants of Newfoundland, the Beothuks, were completely wiped out, their folk tales and legends have been lost forever. Newfoundland's oral tradition therefore dates back to the first European settlers. Because Newfoundland was the first part of what is now Canada to be touched by European colonization, its oral tradition is the oldest of Canada's non-Native cultures.

Most of Newfoundland's folk tales were already old by the time they reached the island. Over the years of being told and re-told in outport communities, they gained a distinctive Newfoundland flavour. In a large body of these stories the protagonist is a character named Jack. Sometimes he is lazy or mischievous, but he is nearly always resourceful when faced with adversity. Besides giants and other formidable adversaries, Jack is sometimes confronted with ghosts. The following stories are abridged versions of two Newfoundland folk tales.

Jack the Sailor

Once upon a time, and a very good time it was, in olden times when quart bottles held half a gallon, and houses were papered with pancakes, and pigs ran around with forks stuck in their arse for anyone who wanted a piece of pork, there was this old woman who had a son named Jack. He was going to school, and the old woman couldn't afford to get him nice things for lunch. One day she made him a nice cake, and the other boys snatched it away from him. Jack got mad and took a knife and drove it into one of the boys, so he had to leave town.

The old woman packed his few clothes in a red handkerchief, and Jack started off. He came to a seaport town, and there were some of King George's vessels alongside the dock. He got a job on one of them.

Once a week, you had to appear on deck clean and decent. Jack didn't have any clean clothes, so he didn't look very good. The next week he was even worse. So the skipper had him put ashore on an island with just a bit of bread. Jack said to himself, "Well, the old woman always said I would come to some bad end, and I guess I will too."

Jack laid down for a nap, and when he woke up he said, "Jesus, I must look around and see if anybody lives here." So he walked along until he met an old feller man who was picking up rocks, looking for samples. This old man gave Jack a note and sent him home to his wife.

Well, at the time, while the old man was away, the old woman had the clerk of the town in. They had a couple of bottles of wine and a few ducks, and they were going to have a big treat and quite a time. But then Jack showed up at the door with the note, and the old woman was kind of put out. So she sent him up to the loft to have a sleep. Jack took out his knife and used it to cut open a knothole so he could see what was going on down below.

Soon the old man came home, and when he knocked, the old woman was a long time coming to open the door. When she opened the door, the old man asked her what took her so long, and she said, "I was darning a patch on your old pants."

Then the old man asked, "Did you see any sailor feller come here?"

The old woman said, "Yes, and I sent him up to the loft for a nap."

So the old man shouted out, "Hey up there!" But Jack didn't answer. So the old man shouted, "Sailor ahoy!"

And by-and-by Jack came down and said, "Hello there. I was just dreaming that I was out in a heavy southeaster, taking in the main royals [sails]."

The old man said, "I glory talking to you sailor fellers, cause there's no men like youse." So they told each other a few yarns, and then the old man said, "I heard that you sailor fellers could conjure."

Now Jack had seen everything that went on in the house through the knothole, and he knew where everything was hid. So he said, "Oh Jesus, yes, sailors can conjure. But 'tis awful wicked, you know."

Well, the old man said, "If we had a few bottles of wine and some ducks, we could have a damn good time."

So Jack said, "'Tis alright to conjure, but by Jesus, you'll have the devil out."

The old man said, "I don't give a good goddamn. We'll get a few bottles of wine, and then we'll put him out anyway."

So Jack said, "Now buddy, look in the oven." The old man did, and found the ducks in there.

Then Jack said, "The wine is in that cupboard, but so is the devil. You stand there at the door with the poker, and I'll open the cupboard. When he runs out, you take a sweep at him."

So Jack opened the cupboard, and out ran the clerk of the town. He went straight for the door and ran outside. The old man swung at him with the poker, but all he hit was the door. "My God!" he cried. "That looked like the clerk of the town!"

Jack said, "Jeez! Compare the clerk of the town to the devil, and you'll be hung tomorrow!"

The old man said, "Oh, to hell with 'em!" And they sat down and drank the night through. And then Jack said that he wanted to get off the island. So the old man gave Jack a boat and a sail.

Jack set off, and by-and-by he came to big town where there was a king's castle. But nobody could ever stay in because it was haunted. If you could stay in it, you would get a lot of money. Jack decided he would try it.

The first night he slept there, he was having a mug of tea, when a hairy little man came in. Jack said, "Hello, father. Where did you come from?"

The hairy little man didn't answer. So Jack said, "This will never do." He put the poker in the stove and made it really hot. The hairy little man disappeared, and Jack didn't see anymore of him that night.

The next day Jack went out and met the king's beautiful daughter, and they had a grand time. She became fond of Jack, and she kicked up a fuss about him spending a second night in the haunted castle, because she was afraid he would be killed. But the same thing happened that had happened the first night. The hairy little man came, and wouldn't speak. When Jack put the poker in the stove, he disappeared.

Nobody had ever stayed in that haunted castle a *third* night, so the princess really kicked up a fuss. But Jack went anyway. He wasn't there long when the hairy little man appeared. "Hello, father," Jack said. "Come again tonight?"

The hairy little man sat in a corner, and by-and-by two more queer little fellows came in and sat in two more corners. So Jack said, "Well Jeez, I'll take the other corner."

Then Jack took the poker from the fire and he drove all three of them off with it. But the first one came back, and this time he spoke. He told Jack, "I came to tell 'ee that the king is my brother. I was murdered here for the money that I got. Those fellers that was here was the ones that murdered me for my money, but they never got it. Nobody but me knows where it is. You have won it. If you take up the planking under that table, you will find three jars of money. One full of gold, one full of silver, and one full of coppers. Give the one full of silver to my brother, and you can have the rest. And you can live here as long as you like."

So Jack dug up the money, and married the king's daughter. They lived happily ever after, and had babies by the basketful.

Brave Jack and the Ghosts

Two brothers named Bill and Jack were great comrades from the time they were children. They wouldn't go to sea unless there were jobs on the ship for both of them. When they returned to port with money in their pockets, they would go into the alehouse for some grog. Jack would drink until his money was gone. When he was sober, he would tell Bill, "We'll go to sea again."

Bill would say, "Ah, nonsense. We'll never get nothing like this."

But Jack would reply, "Ah, if I gets it again, I'll know what to do with it."

This happened several times over, with Jack always drinking all of his money away, unless he got Bill to hold onto some of it for him. Bill was the sensible one. Jack was always a bit reckless.

One day when Jack and Bill were ashore, they were admiring a house. Jack said, "If only we could get into that house."

"Go on with your nonsense, Jack," said Bill. "You know we'd never get in the like of that."

"Ah," said Jack, "you never knows."

A young gentleman came along and said good morning to them. Jack said to him, "I was just sayin' to Bill, if only we could get into that beautiful house."

The young gentleman said, "Well now, Jack. You can have that house if you think you can live in it. No man can live in it for spirits. And everything you can think of is in there."

Jack said to Bill, "There, Bill, I knowed I could get us in." They walked around until it was dark. Then they went into the house and started to play cards. After they played cards for a while, Jack said to Bill, "Take the jug and go draw us a jug of rum."

Bill took the jug down to the cellar to draw a jug of rum. But there was an ugly old fellow down there. So Bill went up without the rum. Jack took the jug and went down and drew some rum. Then he went back up. He and Bill played cards and drank rum until it was time for bed.

They weren't in bed very long when three men came in through a window; two big men and one little fellow. The big ones were beating on the little one, and beating him pretty bad. Jack said, "Get out and help him, Bill."

"Go on, Jack," said Bill, "they'll kill us."

So Jack jumped out of bed in his drawers and went right to the little fellow. He sacked [beat] the two big ones off, and they went out the window. Then Jack turned to speak to the little fellow, but he went out the window in a ball of fire. "Well," said Jack, "he's no man. He won't stop to speak to anybody." And he went back to bed.

The next morning the young gentleman came by the house, thinking Jack and Bill would be dead. But when he saw smoke coming out of the chimney, he walked in and said, "Good morning, Jack."

"Good mornin', young gentleman," said Jack.

"How did you get on here last night?"

"Oh, alright," said Jack. "Only a few rats knockin' in the house."

That night Jack and Bill were playing cards again, and Jack said, "Go down and draw a jug of rum." But Bill wouldn't go.

So Jack went himself, and the ugly old fellow was there. Only this time he was three times as ugly as he had been before, and he was sitting across the cask. But Jack rammed the old rum jug down between his legs, and then drew the rum anyway. He went back upstairs, and he and Bill played cards and drank rum until bedtime.

They weren't in bed very long, when those three came in through the window again. Once again, the two big ones were beating on the little one. Jack said to Bill, "Get out and help him. He might speak to you. He won't speak to me."

But Bill said, "Go on, Jack. They'll kill us."

So Jack jumped out of bed in his drawers again, and went right to the little fellow. He sacked off the two big ones, but when he turned to the little fellow, he went out the window again in a ball of fire. Once again Jack said, "He's no man. He won't stop to speak to anybody." Then he went back to bed.

The young gentleman came around again the next morning, expecting to find Jack and Bill dead. But there they were still alive, and Jack said they only heard a few rats knocking around the house. That night Jack and Bill were playing cards again, and Jack said, "Bill, let's go draw a jug of rum."

Bill wouldn't go, so Jack went by himself. There was that ugly old fellow sitting on the cask again, and this time he was *five* times as ugly as he had been before. Jack went to ram the jug down between his legs, but the ugly little fellow wouldn't let him. So Jack upped with his fist and knocked him off the cask. Then he drew a jug of rum. He went back up, and he and Bill played cards and drank rum until bedtime.

They weren't in bed very long before those three men came in through the window again, with the two big ones beating the little one. One again Jack told Bill to get up and help him, and Bill wouldn't. So Jack jumped out in his drawers and went right to the little fellow, and he sacked the two big ones off. When they were gone he turned to the little fellow, and this time the little fellow did not disappear in a ball of fire. He said, "Well now, Jack, 'tis yous I've been fightin' for. If yous'd been like Bill, yous'd been killed."

Then he said, "I'm that young gentleman's father. And them two men killed me. Now you tell him where my bones is at and get him to bury 'em decent."

Jack said, "Well, I'll tell him, but I knows he won't believe me."

"Yes, Jack. He'll believe every word you says." Then the ghost pulled open a drawer and hauled out twelve crocks of silver. He said, "Here's six for you, Jack, and six for the young man."

Then the ghost hauled out twelve crocks of gold and said, "Here's six for you, Jack, and six for the young man."

Jack said, "I'll give them to him, but I knows he won't believe me."

"Yes, Jack, he'll believe every word you says. And tell him of my wish for you to be married to his oldest daughter."

"I'll tell him," said Jack, "but I knows he won't believe me."

"Yes he will, Jack. He'll believe every word you says." The ghost disappeared, and Jack and Bill went to bed.

The next morning the young gentleman came around, expecting to find Jack and Bill dead. But there they were alive, so he asked them how things went the night before.

"Alright," Jack said. "I seen your father here last night."

"Did ya?" said the young man.

"Yes," said Jack. "He was tellin' me about the two men that killed him, and told me where his bones is at, and told me to tell you to get them and bury 'em decent. But I told him you wouldn't believe me."

The young gentleman said, "Jack, I'll believe every word you says."

So Jack hauled out the twelve crocks of silver and said, "There's six for you and six for me." Then he hauled out the twelve crocks of gold and said, "There's six for you and six for me."

Then Jack said, "Your father told me how he wished for me to be married to your oldest daughter. But I told him you wouldn't believe me."

The young gentleman said, "Jack, I'll believe every word you says."

So Jack married the eldest daughter. And because he and Bill were great comrades from the time they were children, he got Bill married to her sister. And they lived happily, They had children by the basketful, and hove 'em outdoors in shelf-fulls, and sent 'em to sea to make sea pies.

A Ghostly Ballad

The province of Newfoundland and Labrador is renowned for its ballads about ships, mariners, and the sea. But shipwrecks and brave fishermen weren't the only subjects that inspired outport balladeers. Among other stories put to rhyme and music were haunting tales of the supernatural. The author of this traditional ballad is not known, but the song dates back to the nineteenth century and is based on an eighteenth-century Scottish ballad, "Fair Margaret and Sweet William." It tells of a young woman who takes her own life after she sees the young man she loves married to someone else. That same night, her ghost appears to the young man to take him away with her in death.

Fair Marjorie's Ghost

Fair Marjorie was sitting in her bower chamber window
A-combing back her hair,
It was there she saw young Willie and his bride
A-climbing the upper church stair.

She drew her ivory comb out of her hair
And flashed it across the floor,
It was out of the bower chamber window she jumped,
She was never to be seen anymore.

About the middle part of the night
When all were fast asleep,
Fair Marjorie appeared in Willie's bedroom
And stood there at his feet.

"Oh, how do you like your blanket," she said,
"And how do you like your sheet,
And how do you like your new married bride
Who lies in your arms asleep?"

"Very well I like my blanket," he said,
"Very well I like my sheet,
But better do I like fair Marjorie
As she stands there at my feet."

She took the ivory comb out of her hair
And smote him across the breast,
Saying, "Be prepared and come along with me
To find your final rest."

He kissed her once and he kissed her twice,
And he kissed her three times o'er,
And then he fell there at her feet
To kiss a woman never more.

Mischievous Fairies

According to legend, when the English, Irish, Scots, and Welsh emigrated to Atlantic Canada, the wee folk of their native isles followed them. Whether we call them leprechauns, "little people," or fairies, they made themselves at home in Newfoundland, Nova Scotia, and Prince Edward Island. The following narrative was recorded by folklorist Barbara Rieti in her book *Strange Terrain*. The narrator is a man from the small community of Colinet, at the head of St. Mary's Bay. Is the story a product of his imagination, or is it the truth?

It was March 1940. It was raining hard that night. Now I had no oil clothes or nothing, but still I was as dry as I am right now sitting here at this table. I left Mt. Carmel four o'clock in the morning. I came to Colinet and travelled across the ice to John's Pond. I was on my way home from John's Pond to North Harbour and it was at the Beaver Pond that the fairies attacked me and took control of the horse. Whatever way I'd turn her, she'd head back toward John's Pond. The fairies would not let the horse leave the pond. So I tied the horse to a stump of a tree on the side of the pond. And you should hear the gibberish and singing all around me. It nearly sent me batty. No man would believe the singing, dancing, and music of these fairy characters. They were so handy they were within reach. When the cloud left, I put my head close to the water, and I saw little things on the side of the bank, around eighteen inches high, like rabbits. I tried to catch them, but they played all around me. They were teasing me. So I said, "Have your way, ye damn things." I left them alone and went back and lay on the sled. I was going to stay the night. I stayed for so long I couldn't stand it anymore. No prayer was any good. So I made oaths and swore on them. It was just like an orphanage when I started swearing. Such crying and screeching you could hear as the little creatures left and went eastward. The horse's eyes lit up the pond. When I finally got home, I untackled the mare from the sled and instead of going to the barn she headed right back up the hill again. I was from four o'clock until six o'clock in the rain, but me cravat didn't have a speck of rain. After that the horse couldn't be held going across the pond. Others wouldn't ride her at all on the pond because she travelled so fast. Once she got off the pond, she was back to her own pace again.

Case Files: The Old Hag

Long before Hollywood ever dreamed up Freddy Kruger, the demonic boogeyman in the *Nightmare on Elm Street* movies, Newfoundlanders had the Old Hag. In terms of fear factor, ugly Freddy actually pales in comparison to the Old Hag. For all his nastiness, Freddy is but a work of fiction. He is scary for two hours on a movie screen. The Old Hag touches the soul much more deeply and darkly.

According to medical science, Old Hag syndrome is a nocturnal phenomenon that can involve feelings of suffocation and paralysis, strong smells, loud noises, and the appearance of apparitions. These are always accompanied by intense fear. Doctors have labelled it as *sleep paralysis* and *night terrors*. As a recognized medical condition, the Old Hag dates back to the ancient Greek physician Galen, who attributed it to indigestion. Folklorists have connected the Old Hag to the Old Norse *mara*, which was a type of demon, and the origin of the English term "nightmare." There have also been connections made to the ancient belief in demons called incubus (male) and succubus (female) that sexually assault young men and women in their sleep. The name comes from a centuries old belief that a witch or hag would sit on the sleeper's chest, making it impossible for the person to breath.

Studies have shown that about 15 percent of all adults in the world suffer at least one Old Hag attack, and it can occur in the daytime as well as at night. Old Hag attacks can have a variety of characteristics, but in a typical episode the sleeper awakes suddenly, feeling a weight on the chest. The victim is unable to move or scream, and is overcome with panic. This period of terror may last only a few seconds, but seems much longer. Sometimes the victim hears phantom footsteps or heavy breathing, sees monstrous shapes or glowing red eyes, smells offensive odours, or senses a malevolent presence in the room. Female victims can experience a horror of being raped. The attack ends as abruptly as it began, and leaves the victim feeling emotionally and physically drained. Repeated attacks can bring about a psychological fear of sleep.

Medical science has theorized that during sleep, the brain releases chemicals that shut the body down so that the sleeper does not physically react to dreams and possibly suffer an injury. Therefore, during an Old Hag attack, the mind is beginning to wake up, but still reacting to the frightening dream, and the body is unable to respond to the sudden need to move or cry out. The victim is caught in a twilight zone between the conscious and the subconscious.

Old Hag syndrome is known all over the world, under a variety of names. But in the English speaking world only in Newfoundland does it still bear the name that probably originated in the British Isles centuries ago. It is quite likely that is because, for many generations, a large portion of Newfoundland's population lived in isolated communities in which old beliefs and traditions survived, while they died away elsewhere. The Old Hag has a firmly established niche in Newfoundland culture. An Ontarian or an Albertan who has had an extremely unpleasant night terror experience, but who has never heard of the term Old Hag, would probably have to go to considerable lengths to describe the experience to someone else. When one Newfoundlander tells another, "I was hagged," the listener usually knows exactly what that person is talking about.

Newfoundland's Old Hag is more than a clinically defined medical condition. It has shadowy links to the supernatural. "Sleep paralysis is the fool medical term," says Newfoundland poet, musician, and mystic Drew MacGillivray, currently residing in Conestogo, Ontario. The definitive book on the subject is *The Terror That Comes in the Night: An Experience — Centered Study of Supernatural Assault Traditions* by David J. Hufford, an American Professor of Folklore at Memorial University in St. John's. Through numerous interviews with people who'd had first-hand Old Hag experiences, Professor Hufford learned that beliefs concerning the Hag varied from place to place, and from one generation to the next.

For example, an elderly man told one of Hufford's students that he had witnessed another man "hag" a woman who had rejected his sexual advances. The man doing the hagging had projected his spirit to the woman's bedroom. When the woman saw the ghost-hag standing over her, she was paralyzed with fear and foamed at the mouth. Only the intervention of her father saved her. He drove the hag off by saying his daughter's name backwards. After that, the woman kept a bottle near her bed, because she knew that if you swung a bottle at the spirit that was hagging you, the spirit would die.

One man told of hearing phantom footsteps and seeing an old woman who turned into a blob of light that resembled an elephant. A female interviewee said that she woke up in her bed with a man on top of her, gripping her wrists and pressing down on her. She could even smell his sweat. Yet another individual said he was sleeping in the afternoon, when he was jarred awake by the sound of a slamming door. He became aware of something pressing down on him and the presence of a murky shape in the room. He had the sense that whatever the shape was, it was evil.

Just as there are measures one can take for protection against other forms of supernatural evil, so are there steps that can be taken to defend oneself against the Old Hag. Professor Hufford learned of one woman who placed a pot of urine under her bed to thwart a neighbour who had been hagging her. The woman who had been doing the hagging was forced to desist, because as long as the pot of urine was under her victim's bed, she herself was unable to urinate.

Going to sleep with a board or a shingle across your chest, with a knife or a nail sticking up from it, was believed to discourage the Hag from sitting on you. Saying your name backwards, that is, last name/first name, could also break the Hag's grip. The victim could also fall back on that reliable shield against evil, the Lord's Prayer. As a final resort, the victim could say the Lord's Prayer backwards, if the person was indeed capable of such a feat.

Is the Old Hag nothing more than a waking nightmare? Is it an attack by a hostile person with supernatural powers? Or is it something

Drawing by Michelle Blackman from a 19th century illustration.

The Old Hag torments a sleeping victim. An Old Hag attack is described by all who have experienced it as absolutely terrifying.

that creeps out of the unknown to strike sleeping victims at random? Consider the following accounts, and reach your own conclusions.

The Dead Lady and the Night Hag

Many accounts of hauntings, particularly those that involve poltergeist activity, describe loud noises such as knocking, slamming doors, and pots and pans banging together. These noises are dramatic and can be frightening to those who hear them because they seem to come out of nowhere. But a sound much more subtle than a clanging, banging racket can also be a source of genuine terror.

Imagine you are in bed at night, alone in the room, with no other sound but that of your own breathing. Then you hear a sigh of breath that is not yours! Imagine being confronted with something "just made of darkness." This story was contributed by Sean Clarke of St. John's, in February 2010.

Part I, age 19, Summer 2001

I was living in St. John's with a girlfriend in an apartment that was supposedly built on an old scrap yard (according to her, and she wasn't sure at all). The building was very old with multiple stages of repair and renovations over the years evident. I was just back for the summer, though I had big hopes of staying with this woman permanently.

I was alone, sleeping on the couch in our living room. She was working at a bar. I was half-asleep, in a weird stage of sleep when I would have the worst nightmares happen. I looked into the hall. This looked completely real.

I saw a dark figure standing there, half-obscured by a wall. It was hooded and approximately seven feet tall. Besides that it was just made of darkness. It was so dark. It's hard to find words for this description. Anyway, it just stood there, staring at me, not moving at all. I was locked in eye contact with it, though I could not see any eyes to speak of. I was horrifically afraid. I felt like a freezing weight was crushing me. I could not move or breathe. It felt like it lasted for a very long time, then I snapped out of it, turned a light on, turned the television on, and smoked cigarettes until my girlfriend got home. I only felt safe sleeping in her arms in that apartment after that, as if love was some kind of repellent to it. She never saw it; I never told her of it. If I had to sleep alone in that apartment after that it was in our room with the main ceiling light on.

I do not recall ever seeing anything like it before or since. I have described it to other folks here, mostly acquaintances of mine. Some called it the Night Hag.

This is the only city that I have ever had paranormal problems in.

Part 2, age 27, 2009–2010

I just moved out of this house (the Dead Lady did severely scare me, but I left for other reasons). It is a split level home. We had the front; the landlord had the back. The house was built in 1965 (according to the landlord) and our city is over five hundred years old with a history of genocide against the local Native population, the Beothuks, who are now extinct, as well as a history of seemingly endless wars, both foreign and domestic, and poverty. Our province is almost exclusively Irish (genetically) with some English. Any others are recent arrivals and are still a tiny minority.

I was there in that house for three months, with two other male roommates. Two of us are cousins who only recently returned here to our home city from other, faraway parts of Canada. One of us is an Albertan friend of my cousin's. We all worked together doing security at a nightclub. I recently left work due to an injury. That is when I heard her breath, when I was spending more time alone in that house.

I got cold shivers sometimes when I was alone in that house. I felt that there was another person in my presence, but I could not explain it.

Then I was trying to sleep in our living room one night. I was home alone. I was facing the wall, lying on a couch. There was no music or television playing. There were no animals present in the house at the time. There was only the sound of my own breathing pattern. I was lying there, trying to sleep, listening to my own breathing, in and out, in and out. Then I heard a breath that was not mine. It was loud and obvious. It was out of sync and it came from approximately a meter behind me. I sat up, turned on a light, turned the television on, and tried my best to not show any fear. That was when I stopped sleeping when I was alone in that house. I have a history of post-traumatic stress disorder, depression, and insomnia. This situation severely aggravated my insomnia. I was a paramedic for five years. My career ended two years ago. I have severe nightmares about car accidents, a dead baby, and people screaming and begging for their lives. This was not one of those dreams: I was not asleep.

Then I heard her again. There was no non-living presence there.

Another time, I was home with my Albertan roommate, whom I will refer to as J (I will refer to my cousin as R). We were sitting in our living room by ourselves watching television, J and I. I walked up the short staircase upstairs to the bathroom. I walked by J's room, where the light was turned on. It was well-lit up. I was looking forward, toward the bathroom. I heard her breath in his room, only one breath like the first time. I laughed loudly and hard, and immediately yelled downstairs to J about what had just happened, again trying to hide my fear. I used the washroom before going back downstairs.

I was sober as a judge for both of these events.

I also felt her sit on the couch when I was sleeping, like a weight compressing the couch that wasn't mine. I was home alone when this occurred. I never understood the significance of this occurrence when it happened. I thought my mind was playing tricks on me. That was before the breathing incidents.

R has had multiple encounters with the Dead Lady. Most of them involved doors opening and closing by themselves. The house was slightly drafty, but you can tell the difference between slight movement and actual, full opening and closing of doors. He saw a doorknob twist by itself just as he was about to open the door. He saw a crawlspace door open and shut on its own. After that, he nailed the crawlspace door shut and nailed a towel over it. He is a happy go lucky type and he just basically says, "Screw it. It can't hurt me."

Except for the time he and J drew knives and yelled to me to wake me up. We had just moved in when this occurred. I was heavily sedated (for sleeping) when this occurred. I woke up, left my room, saw them there, told them to not wake me again, and went back to bed. I had no idea what was going on at the time. This was the first incident with the Dead Lady.

J had the same couch/sleeping/foreign-weight-compression scenario happen to him that had happened to me, except he smelled old women's perfume at the same time. He saw the crawlspace door incidents that R saw. J had similar shivers and foreign presence feelings as I did. J ran screaming into the middle of our street one night. J is severely scared by all this.

✝

I have done some research on The Night Hag since I wrote the above excerpts. It is a common phenomenon here in St. John's. I don't know if the thing I saw in Part 1 was a Night Hag, but I have never been more terrified, and I have literally lived the stuff of nightmares.

If you want to experience a paranormal event, find an old house or apartment in downtown St. John's, rent it for a month, and sleep in it alone in total darkness every night for the duration of your stay there. I would never wish the Night Hag or whatever it was that I saw on anyone, but you have to see it to believe it.

They say it eats a piece of your soul when you see it. I believe it. It's something I'll never forget.

Gene Browne's Old Hag

I was sleeping one night when I had this dream that I was walking up to this house that I recognized, but have never seen before; I guess one of the things that occurs in a dream. So I get up to the door, and a guy and his two sisters answered; three people I have never seen before, but was really good friends with in this dream. They invited me in and told me to wait in the living room while they went to get ready. I still remember every detail of the house. When you walk in, there was a hallway to the kitchen, and to the left was a turnoff for another very short hallway to the living room. In the room there was a window dead center, a couch to the left, and a chair to the right. I sat in the chair. Their mother walked in and sat across from me on the couch. She was small, with curly hair and glasses.

We were just speaking like a mother and family friend would, when I heard the shutters just slam on the window to my right. It was unexpected and loud, so I closed my eyes and when I opened them, the mother was on my chest and had my arms folded over, she'd caught me in a scared position. She was turned into this thing with razor sharp teeth, and the strength was unbelievable. I was pushing and pushing her off my chest and she wasn't moving, and I'm no small dude. She was about an inch away from me, just screaming like a banshee, just roaring in my face. It was terrifying. I remember lying in my bed and being half in the dream world and half out of it. I could see my bedroom and the dream at the same time. I couldn't sing out to anyone for help. I was basically just feeling terrorized for what seemed to be ten minutes, but was probably more like thirty seconds.

When I woke up and went out, my ears were actually ringing and my whole body was sore, like the kind of sore after you've experienced something terrifying. My nerve endings were shot. It was a pretty real experience, since I had some physical after effects from it.

Tom's Story

My search for stories about the Old Hag brought about a telephone conversation with Tom, who is in his seventies. Tom said that when he was young, he used to get hagged quite often. "It was an awful thing," he said. "It used to scare the Jesus out of me." However, it was Tom's father whose tendency to "get hagged" resulted in an incident that Tom laughs about today, although it probably wasn't very funny to the other people involved at the time. This is Tom's Old Hag story

We could always tell when Dad was being hagged, because of the queer sounds that would come out of him. He'd be in bed asleep, and the sounds he made were awful. They'd stand your hair on end.

One day me and Dad and a friend of mine named Alec went out hunting. We were gonna spend the night at me brother Walter's house. But Walter didn't know we were coming. He and his wife Beatrice were gone away. When me and dad and Alec got there, there was nobody home and the door was locked. So I went in through a window. We stayed the night, and in the morning Walter and Beatrice still weren't back.

Dad was asleep in a room upstairs. We could tell from the noises that he was being hagged. Alec and me left him up there and went out to go fishing.

Well, while we were gone, didn't Walter and his wife come home! They didn't know that anyone was in the house. They heard these awful noises coming from upstairs and they didn't know what was going on. They were too friggin' scared to go up there and look. And all the time it was Dad being hagged. They were still downstairs, scared half to death, when me and Alec came back.

It Didn't Like Me

This Old Hag story comes from Charles, who was born in Newfoundland but now lives in Edmonton.

I used to laugh when people would talk about the Hag. I never used to have dreams that were terrible bad. The worst dreams I had was that I was out naked somewhere, like my old school. There I'd be in the hall with nothing on, and I'd be trying to find a room I could go into before anybody saw me. That was the kind of dream I had. Nothing scary about it.

Then one day, when my wife and I were living in a little second floor apartment in St. John's, I had something happen that changed my mind about the Hag. My wife was in the hospital because she had an operation on her ear. I was just back from seeing her, and I lay down in the parlour for a little sleep. It was late afternoon, and I pulled the drapes closed to make the room a bit dark.

So there I was asleep on the sofa, when the next thing I knew, I was in the kitchen. But I wasn't in there alone. Something else was in that room with me. I couldn't see it, but I knew it was there and I knew it didn't like me. The funny thing was that I actually thought I was awake.

There was an ornament that my wife had on the kitchen wall that said TAKE TIME TO SMELL THE FLOWERS. I remember that I was looking at it when something grabbed hold of my arms and started pushing me. That kitchen had a door that opened onto a little balcony. When I looked, I saw the door open by itself. And then I knew that the thing that was pushing me wanted to shove me right out that door and off the balcony. I tried to fight, but there was no strength in my arms. I had the feeling that this thing wanted to show me it could do whatever it wanted to me, and I couldn't do anything about it.

I woke up back in the parlour on the sofa where I'd lain down. It was still afternoon, but I was as scared as if it was the middle of the night. I was almost scared to go into the kitchen, because I had the feeling that the invisible thing was in there. When I did go in, I saw that the door at the balcony was open. I could swear it was closed before.

You're probably thinking, *oh, he just had a bad dream.* Well, maybe it was. But I never had a dream that seemed so real. I was as surprised as hell when I woke up and I was on the sofa. Sometimes I wonder if I didn't really get up, go in the kitchen. and get shoved by something, and then went back into the parlour.

That was not the only time that happened. Three more times I felt something grab me and start to push me. It always came when I was asleep, and it grabbed my arms. This was all while my wife was in the hospital. After she came home it stopped. I never told her about it because I didn't want to scare her. But ever since then I stopped laughing when people talk about the Hag.

Judy's Story

This story came to me by email from Judy Newhook of Botwood.

✝

Here is the true story of my experience with the Old Hag.

I was privileged to have grown up in the seaport town of Botwood, located in central Newfoundland. My childhood was enriched by family who all lived within a stone's throw of each other. With such a rich heritage came hours of storytelling around the family table. My Granny would cuddle us for hours in her old rocking chair, and her legendary tales always included her experiences with the Old Hag. We would sit there wide-eyed and speechless as she spun her tall tales, always ending with tons of questions for this wise lady.

The Old Hag was brought on by eating too much cheese, she would confess, or drinking fresh cow's cream before going to bed. Amongst other reasons, these were the top two that gave a body the most trouble. The Old Hag could not be in the same rank as a bad dream or even a nightmare, heaven forbid. If you were troubled with the Old Hag, there was always the risk that you would not wake up; after all, you were walking on maddening terrain.

Stories, I thought, told by a gifted woman; that's all they were. I was now grown up; a young filly whose dreams asleep and awake were energized with wildfire and a free spirit.

The day came when I was asked if I would be the Maid of Honour at my best friend's wedding. Months of planning brought us to the final night that she would live on earth as a single woman. Those remaining few hours were celebrated with much gusto, the likes that were never seen before in our little seaport town. In the wee hours of the morning we tumbled into bed exhilarated, the thrill of the coming day utmost in our dreams … but not mine!

I dreamed that we were standing in the garden waiting for the bride to make her grand entrance down the aisle of freshly picked flowers, the sound of the running brook water flowing over pebbles was the only music needed. Love was in the air. In my mystic state I saw a bush move to my left, then all calamity broke loose. The moose was a bull with too many points on his massive rack. He was on a mission, and he ran with that same spirit. The bridal party scattered to the four winds, running for cover from the massive beast who threatened their lives as he charged down the same aisle as the bride. I watched in horror at the destruction that unfolded before my very eyes, but I couldn't move. I was not breathing. Like a statue I watched as the bull charged toward me. I screamed, but no sound came out. I tried to put one foot in front of the other. Nothing moved on my body. I was totally paralyzed. Nothing was functioning; only my bladder. The bull was so close I could see the froth that drooled from his mouth and the steam that came through his nose. He was angry, and all that anger was inches from me. Again I let out a silent scream. Why was no one helping me? Fear consumed me. His razor sharp horns were about to plunge into my body, when suddenly with all my might I began to float. Yeah, you got it; F-L-O-A-T about two feet above the raging bull's head. He terrorized the ground while I looked down in complete safety.

I woke up in a sweat with every scene vivid in my mind. I climbed out of bed, jumping over bodies who complained loudly, but I didn't care. I had one thing on my mind: "Where is my Granny?" Over a steaming hot cup of tea I saw my grandmother's eyes just above the rim looking at me, intense, listening to my story. I shivered, shook, begging her to tell me I was still alive. She took my face in her warm hands, kissed my wet tears away and gently said, "Welcome to the world of the Old Hag. Now girl, make sure you pass down your story. I'm off to bed. Good night."

Just the Hag, Not My Ghost

This story came to me from Donna Barr of Queen's Cove. It describes an incident that occurred when she was a resident of Jackson's Arm. It is the seeming ordinariness of this story that gives it a rather creepy quality.

I rented an older house at the end of a dead end road in Jackson's Arm when I worked at the Cat Arm Hydroelectric Project. It was renovated to cut off the second floor (the staircase was removed), accessed only by a hatch in the porch. My housemate, a nurse who also worked on the project, insisted a ghost lived up there. I investigated the upper floor but didn't find any evidence of anything or anyone moving around up there.

Sometime later my housemate moved out, and I had the house to myself. One night I had a male visitor. I heard the storm door latch, then the inside door open, and someone walk across the house to my bedroom. I even heard "him" walk across the grate of the floor furnace. I looked up to see him leaning against the door jamb with one leg cocked across the other (he was wearing navy track pants with a white stripe down the side of the leg) and his hands in his jacket (a hooded parka) pockets. His hood was up, hiding his face, but I knew he was looking at me. I asked what he wanted. He shook his head, turned around, and left. I heard all the sounds of him leaving over the floor furnace, and doors opening and closing. A couple of minutes after hearing the outside door close, I got up to check. Nobody was outside. This was 1984 or 1985. The house did make funny noises, I have to admit that, but I think it was just the Hag, not my ghost.

A Scratching Noise

Frank Pottle of St. John's submitted this rather unnerving account of an Old Hag experience.

✝

I have experienced the Old Hag a few times. There was a period for about two years where I would have these experiences every couple of months. It happened at my home and at work. It's a completely terrifying experience, especially when it happens for the first time. Some people feel intense pressure on their chest and actually see the Old Hag sitting on them or standing in the room somewhere. In my episodes, I saw nothing. I only heard things around me. In each case I was always frozen in place.

Paralyzed. I couldn't scream or move, and I would try with every ounce of power in me. All I could do was move my eyes around.

The scariest incident for me was when I was lying in my bed. I woke up facing towards the centre of my bedroom, my back facing the wall. I was scared as soon as I woke up because I couldn't move or speak. I could see all around my room. I could see the TV, but not hear it since I had it on mute. Everything was as clear as if I had normally awoken. Then I started to hear a scratching noise behind me on the bed sheet: slow and long scratches. It was getting closer and closer to me. I could hear it making it closer and closer to my head. When the scratching noise finally reached my pillow and was directly behind my head, I remembered that my mother suggested the Lord's Prayer when this was happening. So I tried to recite it the best I could. Even though I had been off on a few words it seemed to have worked. I broke away from whatever was holding me there and I got up to turn my lights on. I had them on for the rest of the night.

Courtney's Story

This Old Hag account from a former resident of Labrador came to me courtesy of Matt Massie and the Ghosts of Labrador.

When I was twelve years old I had my first Old Hag encounter. I had a dream that a woman's humming was coming towards me and I was unable to scream out or move my body. I blinked my eyes and the next thing I knew she was on top of me. I could feel her breath hitting my neck. Then I woke up in a sweat and in tears.

When I got to high school I discovered that my experience was an Old Hag dream. During that time I had only had it the few times. However, when I went away to university in Newfoundland I decided to take some folklore classes, which ended up discussing the Old Hag.

It was then that the dreams became more frequent. Almost every night there were times I would wake up screaming and scare the crap out of my roomie. So, with that being said, I will tell you what I experienced.

I awake and I am only able to move my head. The rest of my body is numb. I hear breathing getting deeper and louder, and I see a woman dressed in black with grayish white hair and black for eyes. She has wrinkles on her face. She walks towards me and begins to crawl up me till she reaches my chest. She brings her head down towards my face and just when our faces are about to touch, I awake.

There are times that when I am having the dream, that if I do not see her as soon as I realize I am having it, my eyes will go around the room till I see her, because I can sense her presence. Once I see her, it's like something out of a scary movie. My eyes hit her, and she is immediately right in front of me. Sometimes she is standing over me by the head of my bed. If you read the legends of her, it is claimed that you can only have the dream lying on your back. This is not true. I have experienced it lying on my stomach, which is more messed up because she still gets on top of me, but I can't see her or move my body. Once I am able to wiggle a finger or move even a little bit of some part of my body, I awake.

From my folklore classes I learned that's how you escape the dream, by being able to move a part of your body, even if it is a finger. Her story originates from Newfoundland on Bell Island. The legend of the Old Hag claims that if you are unable to wake up before she gets too close to you, or if you are in the dream too long, you will die. I recently graduated and moved to B.C., and I guess it doesn't matter where I am: I will never be able to truly escape her.

Mysteries of the Sea

The Ghostly Crew of the *Charles Haskell*

In the days of wooden sailing ships, before the arrival of such technological wonders as electric lighting, radar, and wireless radio, collisions at sea were not uncommon. It might seem that on the vast oceans, vessels would have plenty of room in which to maneuver and give each other a wide berth. But navigators tended to stick to relatively narrow, well-known and well-travelled sea lanes. Fishing fleets were drawn to the most productive waters, where large numbers of vessels would be at work, all within sight of each other. The resulting congestion increased the possibility of collision, especially in adverse sailing conditions such as thick fog or heavy seas. One such accident gave rise to the legend of the *Charles Haskell*.

Like many ghost tales, the *Haskell* story has more than one version. In one account, the ship was a Boston schooner. Another says she was out of Salem or Gloucester, Massachusetts. The stories agree that from the beginning, the *Charles Haskell* was cursed. While the schooner was still under construction, a workman was killed when he broke his neck in a fall. Sailors immediately marked the *Haskell* as a bad-luck ship, and refused to sign aboard. The captain who was originally commissioned to take command of her backed out of his contract.

The new ship sat in harbour for a year before Clifford Curtis, a captain who scoffed at superstitions, became the *Haskell*'s master. He was able to round up a like-minded crew, one of whom was a seventeen-year-old

Ghost ships, like the one in this early nineteenth-century illustration, appear in many Newfoundland tales of hauntings at sea.

Nova Scotian named George W. Scott. Early in March of 1866 (or 1871, depending on the version of the story), the *Charles Haskell* sailed from her New England port for the cod-rich waters of the Grand Banks of Newfoundland.

On March 6 or 7, while young Scott and the rest of the crew were preparing to go out in the dories, Captain Curtis saw that a storm was brewing. He decided to take his schooner to the Georges Bank, where he could drop anchor in the relatively shallow water and ride out the blow. Every other skipper in the area had the same idea, including the captain of the schooner *Andrew Jackson*. Scores of vessels were riding the swells within a confined area when hurricane-force winds swept down upon them.

As shrieking winds and mountainous waves battered the ships, the *Charles Haskell* and the *Andrew Jackson* either broke free of their anchor lines, or the captains found it necessary to cut them. With no ground tackle (anchors) to hold them, the schooners were at the mercy of the storm. They collided!

The prow of the *Charles Haskell* struck the *Andrew Jackson* amidships and sliced right through, cutting her in two. The vessel went down in an instant, taking all hands with her. Not a single body was recovered. The *Charles Haskell* was damaged, but remained afloat. None of the crew had been injured. Nonetheless, when the *Haskell* returned to port, George Scott and his shipmates quit. They would not sail on the bad-luck ship again.

Cursing superstitious sailors, Captain Curtis tried to find a new crew. It wasn't easy, with the *Charles Haskell* now doubly cursed. But the following spring, Curtis and the *Haskell* were out on the Grand Banks once again. The ship's course eventually took her to the Georges Bank, to the very spot where the *Andrew Jackson* had gone down. This time the *Haskell* was alone. There wasn't another sail in sight.

It was after midnight, and only two crewmen, Manuel Fernandez and Oscar Roihards, were on deck standing watch, when something happened that would make the bravest sailor's hair stand on end. A dozen or so men came up out of the sea and climbed aboard the *Charles Haskell*! These phantoms were the drowned crew of the *Andrew Jackson*. Their eye sockets were sunken and hollow, their faces grey and gaunt in the moonlight, and their oilskins dripped seawater. They were silent, and did not even seem to be aware of the two terrified crewmen.

Fernandez and Roihards went below and roused Captain Curtis. When they told him what was happening, the skipper must have thought they'd been into the grog. But, at last, he went out on deck to see for himself.

Before the astonished captain and his two men's very eyes, the ghosts of the drowned men went about their sailors' duties. One stood with his hands on the ship's wheel. Some were in the rigging, letting out sails. Others stood at the ship's rails, going through the motions of baiting hooks and tossing out lines.

Soon all of the *Haskell*'s men were awake and on deck, watching the ghostly crew at work. The fact that the spectres did not act in any threatening manner, or even acknowledge the presence of the flesh-and-blood crew, did nothing to abate the men's terror. As far as they were concerned, the hand of death lay upon the *Charles Haskell*.

As dawn approached, the ghosts suddenly stopped their work, went to the railing, and slipped over the side back into the sea. The crew immediately demanded that Curtis take them home. The captain did not argue. But on two more nights, as the *Haskell* was homeward bound, the phantom crew came aboard again, and performed their mariners' tasks.

When the *Charles Haskell* reached home port at last, the entire crew quit. Captain Curtis, no longer a skeptic, swore that he would never sail her again. Indeed, as the story of the ghostly crew spread, other sailors made it clear that they would never so much as set foot on the cursed ship. There was a belief that the ghost of a drowned sailor would return to his ship, if that ship sailed over the place where he had died. Sailors who heard about the haunting of the *Charles Haskell* reasoned that the ghosts of the *Andrew Jackson*'s crew could not return to their ship, because she lay in pieces on the bottom of the sea; instead, they returned to the vessel that had sunk their ship and caused their deaths.

There are conflicting stories about the fate of the *Charles Haskell*. One says that because no sailors would go aboard her, she sat rotting at her mooring until at last she was towed out to sea and burned. Another account says that a firm in Nova Scotia bought the *Haskell*, and used her to haul timber. Her crews reported no further hauntings, but the skippers deliberately avoided the Georges Bank.

In 1874, Proctor Brothers of Gloucester, Massachusetts, published *Fishermen's Ballads and Songs of the Sea*. This collection included a poem by Harry L. Marcy called "The Ghostly Crew." Over the years there have been several slightly varying versions of the poem, under different titles: "The Ghostly Sailors" and "The Ghostly Fishermen." The narrator is a crewman of the *Charles Haskell*, telling the story of the encounter with the dead crew.

> You may smile if you're a mind to
> But perhaps you'll lend an ear
> Like men and boys together
> For nigh on fifty year
> Who have sailed upon the ocean
> In summer's pleasant days
> And through the stormy winters

When the howling winds do rage

I have tossed about on Georges
Been a'fishing in the bay
Down south in early seasons
Most anywhere it would pay
I have been in different vessels
To the Western banks and Grand
Have been in herring vessels
That went to Newfoundland

There I saw storms, I tell you
When times looked very blue
But some ways I've been lucky
And always have got through
I ain't a brag, however
I won't say much, but then
I ain't the easier frightened
Than the most of other men

T'was one night as we were sailing
We were off shore aways
I never shall forget it
In all my mortal days
It was in the grim dark watches
I felt a chilling dread
Come over me as if I heard
One calling from the dead

Right o'er our rail came climbing
All silent, one by one
A dozen dripping sailors
Just wait till I am done
Their faces pale and sea worn
Shone ghostly through the night

Each fellow took his station
Just as if he had the right

They moved around among us
Until land did heave in sight
Or rather I should say so
The lighthouse showed its light
And then those ghostly sailors
All to the rail as one
They vanished like the morning mist
Before the rising sun

We sailed right into harbour
And every mother's son
Will tell you the same story
Just like I have done
The trip before the other
We were on Georges then
Ran down another vessel
And sank her and her men

Those were the same poor fellows
I hope God rests their souls
That our old craft ran under
That night on Georges shoals
So now you have heard my story
It is just as I say
I do believe in spirits
Since that time, anyway.

The Ghost That Wasn't

In the autumn of 1823, a man from Torbay named Robert Brace was first mate on a barque en route from Liverpool, England, to St. John's.

The voyage had been long and rough, and the crew was exhausted. But the Newfoundland coast was in sight, and the men looked forward to reaching port at last.

Brace and the captain made their rounds on deck, and then went into the captain's cabin. They talked briefly, and then the captain went back on deck to see to other duties. He left Brace in the cabin to work out some coordinates on the charts.

Engrossed in his work, Brace glanced up once and noticed someone sitting at the captain's desk, bent over and apparently at work. The first mate assumed that while he had been absorbed in his own task, the captain had come back in without his noticing. Brace finished his work, and then turned to confer with the captain. This time he looked right at the man, and was startled to realize that it wasn't the captain.

Indeed, the man wasn't even a member of the crew! Brace had never seen this man before. Who was he, and how had he gotten aboard a ship that had been at sea for weeks? Was he a stowaway?

Brace immediately told the man to identify himself. The stranger didn't say a word, but looked up at the first mate. Brace could see that the man had been writing on a slate. But what really caught his attention were the stranger's eyes. They looked as cold as ice. It was like staring into the face of death.

No man who went to sea in the days of sail and wooden ships could be called faint of heart, and Brace had faced danger many times. But almost to a man, sailors of that age were superstitious. Something about the stranger's frosty glare struck fear into Robert Brace. For a moment he stood trembling. Then he ran out on deck to find the captain.

The skipper was surprised when Brace anxiously asked him who the man was sitting at his desk, writing on his slate. The captain said it must be the second mate or the steward. No one else in the crew had any business being in the captain's quarters. He also wondered why Brace was shaking like a leaf, as though he had seen a ghost.

Brace told the captain that the man in his cabin was not a member of the crew. He didn't know who the man was at all. Probably suspecting that Brace might be imagining things after the long weeks of heavy seas and little sleep, the captain reminded him that there simply could not be a stranger aboard the ship. But at Brace's insistence, the skipper finally agreed to go back to the cabin with him.

They found no one in the captain's quarters. Not a thing was missing or out of place. The captain might well have still wondered if Brace had been suffering from some sort of delusion. Then the first mate showed him the slate!

Brace had picked it up from the captain's desk. On it was written in clear script, "Sail for the northwest." The handwriting was not the captain's, nor was it Brace's.

The captain left the cabin with the slate in his hand. He compared the handwriting on it with that of every man in the crew who knew how to write. There were no matches. The skipper decided that impossible though it seemed, they had a stowaway aboard. He ordered the crew to search the ship.

The men went through the vessel from bow to stern. They looked into every dark corner below deck where a man might hide, but they found no one. The captain was deeply puzzled. He would have doubted that Brace had really seen the stranger at all, were it not for the writing on the slate. He decided that the only thing for him to do was follow the mysterious instructions. He told the first mate, "Have the helmsman bring her about ninety degrees, Mr. Brace, and point her northwest."

Then the captain gave orders that he wanted the ship's whole company on alert. He sent some men aloft, and stationed others along the rails so that he had eyes covering the sea in every direction. The captain had an uneasy feeling, and no idea of what they might be sailing into. The men were not happy about changing course when they were so near to home, and the whole strange business made them jittery. But they obeyed the captain's orders.

For an hour or so no one on board saw anything unusual. Then a man in the crow's nest cried, "Ice ahead!"

The captain looked and saw that they were approaching a field of icebergs. Of all the hazards to wooden hulled ships, few were more deadly than ice. The towering white monsters that rise above the surface of the sea are but the visible parts of huge masses of ice hidden beneath the waves. The slightest brush against one of those granite-like formations could cave in a ship's hull and send her to the bottom. The men were afraid, but the captain told the helmsman to hold his course.

Two more hours passed, and the packs of ice around the ship thickened. They now encountered a vast field of flat, grinding ice floes. Then from aloft came a cry, "Ship off the port bow!"

There, locked in the ice, was a ship — or at least, the remains of one. The vessel had clearly been badly damaged. The captain had no doubt that the unlucky ship would soon go down. He couldn't see if anybody was aboard and took his vessel as near as he possibly could. Then he told Robert Brace to take a company of men in the ship's boat to investigate.

As Brace and his men neared the stricken vessel, they heard voices. Brace called out, and immediately men appeared at the rail. They waved madly and cried out for help. "Thank God you came! We couldn't have lasted much longer! We're sinking!"

Because of the ice, Brace couldn't take his boat right up to the ship. Instead, he took it to the other side of one of the ice pans that had the doomed ship in its grip. Then he shouted to the imperiled sailors to abandon ship and come across the ice to him. Brace carried out the rescue without losing a single man. The last man to leave the ship was the captain, and it wasn't long after he got off that his ship slipped beneath the dark waters and was gone.

Later, aboard Brace's ship, the captain of the rescued crew explained that he'd been en route from Liverpool to Quebec City, when his ship became icebound. They'd been held in the ice for so long, with their hull buckling, that they'd given themselves up for lost. How was it, he wanted to know, that their ship had miraculously come along to pluck them from the jaws of death?

Brace and his captain hardly knew how to begin answering the question. The other captain might have thought they were crazy if they started talking about a phantom stranger and mysterious writing on a slate. Then, as the rescued sailors were being warmed by hot cups of tea, and took off some of the coats, mufflers, and hats that had hidden their features, Brace was astonished to see the face of the stranger he had seen in the captain's cabin.

Dumbfounded, Brace confronted the man and asked, "Have you ever been aboard this ship before? Have we ever met?"

The man was shaken by his recent ordeal, and clearly confused by the question. "No," he said. "I don't know you, and I have never been on this ship until just now."

Brace was insistent. "I saw you today, just past noon. You were sitting at the captain's desk, writing on his slate. You looked right at me. I went away to get the captain, but when we came back you were gone. It had to be you. Even your clothes are the same."

"You're mistaken," the man argued. "I was on that ship for weeks. Just after noon, when you claim you saw me on this ship, I was asleep. I was so exhausted, I dozed off. I had a strange dream, though I can't recall just what it was about. How could I possibly have been on your ship?"

Brace threw up his arms in frustration. The other men stared at him as though he'd gone mad. Then the captain went to his cabin and returned with two slates. He handed one of them to the sailor, along with a piece of chalk. "Write 'Sail for the northwest,' on this," he said.

By now the man was thoroughly bewildered, but he did as he was asked. He handed the slate back to the captain. The skipper compared the message the man had just written with the one Brace had found hours earlier. The handwriting was identical! The captain showed both the slates to the sailor.

For a few moments the man stood in stunned silence. Then he said, "Now I recall something of the dream I had this afternoon. I dreamt that I was on another ship, pleading for help."

The only explanation was that somehow, while he slept on board the doomed ship, the desperate sailor's spirit or mind had been transported across the icy waters to the only vessel that could come to the rescue. In an eerie, dramatic way, the sleeping sailor had effectively made a distress call. Robert Brace had not seen a ghost, but a phantom-like projection from a man who was on the brink of death.

Tale of a Haunted Ship

To go aloft amidst the spars and rigging of a tall ship on a rolling sea was dangerous work, even for a sailor with nerves of steel and the nimbleness of a monkey. Falls were among the most common causes of accidental injury and death among sailors. A vessel upon which a man had been killed in an accident was often marked as a bad-luck ship, and a captain could have a difficult time recruiting a crew. The situation was even worse when the ghost of the deceased remained on the ship. The following story appeared in the St. John's *Daily News*, November 15, 1898.

The Yarn of Sailors on a Vessel Lying at Pictou — Who Say the Craft Is Haunted Men Feared to Go Aloft — In Fact They Would Do Nothing — Without Trembling and Left as Soon as Possible.

Joseph Fraser and eight companions tell an interesting story of a vessel lying at Pictou.

The nine men together with the captain, steward and mate, formed the crew of the vessel. She is an old boat, one of the phantom ship character, and the men say she is haunted. All tell the same story regarding certain funny happenings on board and when she reached port, they left her in a hurry. The captain, who seemed to take the matter more coolly than the rest of his crew, endeavoured to induce the men to change their minds, but they turned a deaf ear to all his offers.

The story of the ghost dates back to a former voyage of the vessel. The captain is the only man aboard who knows the history of the tragedy in its fullness, and he is loath to tell all he does know. Half of the yarn is known to the men. It appears that a former sailmaker was sent aloft one stormy night to repair a sail and, when the vessel lurched in a heavy sea, he was thrown to the deck and striking on his head broke his neck. Since then the vessel has been haunted.

The last trip seems to have been worse than any previous one, and the crew solemnly affirm that they were afraid to venture on deck after dark. None would go aloft to trim sail and the men were thoroughly terrified by the strange happenings. Fraser and his companion Williams state that on several occasions when aloft at their work a headless man stood beside them sewing at the sails. It is unnecessary to say that the sailors lost no time in reaching deck by the shortest route. They fairly tumbled down and refused to go aloft again. The captain was asked to explain but simply contented himself with laughing the matter off.

On another occasion the man at the wheel went asleep at his post and was awakened by a strange noise. His cries attracted his comrades, who, rushing from the forecastle, saw the same headless man standing nearby. The second mate made a run for the stranger, but it disappeared like a flash. After that the men refused to go to the wheel unless in pairs and the watches were looked upon with dread.

But the climax was capped when one night the compass turned about. The captain then became excited and for over an hour it was impossible to tell which way the vessel was heading. In about an hour the instrument resumed its normal condition, but the men became so restless that they almost mutinied. When the vessel left Pictou they refused to go any further in her and have been shipped at this port.

Samson's Island Ghost

This item was provided by Beverly Warford, the public librarian at Point Leamington. In the newspaper article that follows her introduction, look for the rather casual mention of a haunting, amidst the reporting of ordinary community news, such as the arrivals of vessels in port and the building of a new parsonage.

Over the last 12 years, I have spent considerable time researching the genealogy and history of the Exploits District. These [stories] have been transcribed and posted to the Newfoundland and Labrador GenWeb where I am co-coordinator for the Exploits District.… Below is an article from Lewisporte from Oct 4, 1905, and an interesting ghost story.

Lewisporte

Oct 4 — Speaking generally Lewisporte life has been very quiet during the past summer, this being the excuse your correspondent has to offer for his long silence.

Very little shipping has been done to date in consequence of which there is a very large accumulation of lumber here awaiting transportation. Presumably the Timber Estate directors are more concerned in negotiating the prospective Pearson deal than in shipping lumber. There is, however, a little stir now in the lumber element, the good ship Hora having just arrived to load a cargo for the South American market. This vessel will take about one million feet, but it will take several such vessels to clean up the lumber yard.

The schooner Poppy, Edward WHITELEY, master, from Bonne Esperance, bound to St. John's, encountered a north-east storm on Saturday the 30th, and put in there in a disabled condition. On board the vessel were 55 of WHITELEY's fishermen, returning home from their summer's operations, who report a hard experience in the storm. They were across NDB near Black Island when suddenly the jumpstay broke, in consequence of which the mainmast very soon went by the board, and as the little craft was labouring very heavily it was difficult to clear away the wreckage and get her in sailing trim again.

However, they got her in here safely, minus the mainmast, no one being the worse for the rough experience. Your correspondent interviewed the master who avers that a strange incident occurred whilst the vessel was anchored at Samson's Island on Sunday night, says that by some unseen and unaccountable means the anchor chain were being hauled up, the pump set working, and the wheel manipulated as if the vessel were being got under way. The Samson's Island people attribute the phenomena to a proverbial ghost which haunts the Island. Thirty-five of the men left here by train for St. John's.

The Methodist people, nothing daunted, are advising ways and means to build another parsonage to replace the one burnt last spring. Fortunately there was some insurance on the burnt building which will afford considerable help financially. The Rev. Mr. BLUNT is busying himself in the interest of his circuit and finds his hands full in attending to the various demands on his attention. The Methodist cause has in Mr. BLUNT an energetic, capable and promising addition to the ministerial ranks.

The Orange Order here is pushing itself into a prominent position; a capacious hall is nearing completion which will be a credit to the Order and will supply the need of a place for meetings of a public character.

Mr. Allan HAYWARD of Musgrave Harbour, has been duly installed as "domine" of the schools. His initial work creates favourable impressions and gives promise of success.

A Mystery of the Gulf

The waters of the Gulf of St. Lawrence were hazardous for wooden sailing ships. From the earliest days of European exploration, ice, fog, tricky currents, and raging storms made the region a graveyard for vessels and the men who sailed in them. A legend grew in the lore of generations of mariners about mysterious lights that were seen in various locations from the coast of New Brunswick to the shores of Newfoundland. These "phenomenal lights" were often seen just before major storms, and came to be dreaded as harbingers of death and disaster. But what were they?

Today's meteorologists cite atmospheric anomalies as the source of the strange lights. In 1880 a historian named Welcome A. Greene theorized that phosphorescent fish called menhaden, which travel in schools of millions, were the cause. But in the late eighteenth and early nineteenth centuries, it was believed that the lights were supernatural manifestations, ghost ships, or the souls of drowned sailors. Whatever they were, they struck fear into the hearts of fishermen, merchant sailors, and navy swabs from Baie des Chaleurs to Cape Race. The ghostly lights might even have played a significant role in the calamity that befell a mighty British armada that sailed against New France in 1711. The following article, titled "A Mystery of the Gulf," appeared in the *Daily Advertiser* of London, Upper Canada (Ontario), in September 1828:

A Mystery of the Gulf
What the Phenomenal Lights Seen in the Lower St. Lawrence Portend to the Canadian Fishers

Miramichi, N.B., August 27 — The mysterious lights in the Gulf and the Lower St. Lawrence, those sure precursors of a tempestuous fall with grievous shipwrecks, have been unusually brilliant this season. The light off the Cape Maria Cascapediac has blazed almost every night since May 15. In the Baie des Chaleurs, the Point Mizuenette light has been seen nightly by hundreds of people from the settlements of New Bandon, Grande Anse, Caraquette and Salmon Beach. The *habitant* say they are supernatural manifestations marking scenes of wreck and murder, or warning the sailor of great tempests; while the English settlers think they are the will-o'-the wisps of the ocean. Whatever they may be, it is a fact established by the experience of a century that when they blaze brightly in the summer nights the fall is invariably marked by great storms. One would think on looking at these mysteries from the shore that a ship was on fire. The heavens behind are bright and the clouds above silvered by the reflection. The sea for half a mile is covered with a sheen as of phosphorous. The fire itself seems to consist of blue and yellow flames, now dancing high above the water, and then flickering, paling and dying out only to spring up again with fresh brilliancy. If a boat approaches it flits away, moving further out, and the bold visitor pursues in vain. At the first streak of daylight it vanishes in the form of a mist, and is seen no more until darkness again sets in. These lights are brightest when there is a heavy dew, and are plainly visible from the shore from midnight until two in the morning. They appear to come in from the sea shoreward, and at dawn retire gradually and are lost in the morning fog.

Paradis, the French pilot who took charge of the British fleet under Admiral Sir Hovenden Walker when it sailed up the St. Lawrence from Boston to seize Quebec in 1711, declared he saw one of these lights just before the armada was shattered on the 22nd of August: in fact, he said it danced before his vessel, the *Neptune,* all the way up the Gulf. Walker's squadron comprised the flagship *Edgar,* 70 guns; the *Windsor,* 60 guns; the *Montague,* 60 guns; the *Swiftshire,* 70 guns; the *Monmouth,* 70 guns; the *Dunkirk,* 60 guns; the *Humber,* 80 guns; the *Sunderland,* 60 guns; the *Devonshire,* 80 guns; the *Enterprise,* 40 guns; the *Sapphire,* 40 guns; the *Kingston,* 60 guns; the *Leonard,* 54 guns, and the *Chester,* 50 guns; with no less than seventy transports, of which the *Despatch, Four Friends, Francis, John and Hannah, Henrietta, Blessing,*

Antelope, Hanna and Elizabeth, Friend's Adventure, Rebecca, Martha and Hanna, Johanna, Unity and *Newcastle* were from New England ports. On leaving Boston Sir Hovenden drew from Governor Dudley rations for 9,385 Englishmen, seamen and soldiers, and 1,786 colonists on board the fleet. On the 20th August when they lay off Egg Island, on the north shore of the St. Lawrence, Having just cleared Gaspe Bay, a dense fog fell upon them. The Admiral ordered the vessels to keep together, and soundings were taken every half hour, but the land gave no bottom. On the night of the 22nd Paradis lost his head and signalled for the fleet to close upon the shore. While they were moving slowly a dreadful gale arose and as Sir Hovenden said in his journal which was published in London in 1720: "We soon found ourselves amongst rocks and small islands, fifteen leagues further than the log gave, when the whole fleet had like to have been lost." "But by God's good providence," he goes on, "all the men-of-war, though with extreme hazard and difficulty, escaped. Eight transports were cast away and had I not made the signals as I did, but continued sailing, it is a great question whether any ship or men had been saved." After the wreck the roster showed only 8,878 survivors. The Labrador shore, says the historian Charlevoix, was strewn with the bodies of the Royal Guards and many more of Marlborough's veterans, whose corpses were easily distinguishable by their scarlet coats. It was suspected that Paradis had willfully cast the fleet away. In his defence, as found in the writings of Mere Juchereau, he pleaded that he saw the moving lights when they first made Gaspe Bay and told some of the high officers that heaven had ordained a terrible catastrophe, "so clearly and with such vividness did the celestial fires burn not only by night but often when there was a fog throughout the day." The disaster saved Canada to France for the time being, and the pious colonists reared many churches in gratitude to Notre Dame des Victoires. The court of Queen Anne went into mourning, and Sir Hovenden exiled himself to South Carolina, where, as a French writer quaintly said, "he wrote humorous apologies for the disaster with which God had been pleased to visit the English fleet." The flagship *Edgar*, with 470 men, blew up at Portsmouth on her return from the Gulf, which was "further evidence of God's displeasure at the invasion of New France."

Every great wreck that has taken place since Sir Hovenden's calamity has been preceded, if tradition is to be believed, by these mysterious lights; or rather they have warned the mariner of the fatal storm. When the Gulf gives up its dead there will be a vast muster. In 1797 the French war-ship *La Tribune* was lost, with 300 souls. In 1805 the British transport *Nacas* went down, with 800. In 1831 the emigrant ship *Lady Sherbrooke*, from Derry to Quebec, was lost, only 32 out of 273 passengers being saved. In 1847 nearly 200 Irish emigrants were lost with the big *Carrick*, and 240 more on the *Exmouth*. Two hundred and twenty-five souls perished in the wreck of the *Hungarian* on the 19th February, 1860; 35 on *Canadian* on the 4th of June, 1861, and 237 when the *Anglo-Saxon* was lost in a fog off Cape Race on the 27th April, 1863. How many fishing boats and coasters have gone down with all hands, leaving no sign, it is not safe even to guess. This fall, if the lights are to be believed — and the Gulf fishermen say they cannot lie — storms of unexampled fierceness will rage from the autumnal equinox until winter is past. Should this augury be fulfilled perhaps it may be worthwhile for meteorologists and seafaring men to inquire into the source and origin of these strange watchmen of the deep.

It is worth noting that in November 1828 the ship *Granicus*, bound from Quebec City for Cork, Ireland, foundered in the Gulf and was wrecked on the eastern shore of Anticosti Island. This resulted in one of the most mysterious shipwrecks in Canadian history. About thirty people, including two women and three children, made it to shore, but by the time sailors from a whaling boat found them the following May, they were all dead. The sailors found clear evidence of murder and cannibalism.

Harry Smith of the *Falcon*

There are many accounts of people who have claimed that they've seen someone in a specific location, only to learn later that the individual had actually died. Most amazing is that the death occurred at the very time that

the deceased was "seen" elsewhere. One such incident involved the famed Arctic explorer, Captain Robert Bartlett (1875–1946), a native of Brigus, Newfoundland.

A newspaper reporter once asked Bartlett if he believed in ghosts. Bartlett replied, "Well, sometimes I do and sometimes I don't." In his expeditions to the frontiers of the Far

Captain Robert Bartlett, Newfoundland's famous Arctic explorer, when asked if he believed in ghosts, replied, "Well, sometimes I do and sometimes I don't."

North, Bartlett had been in many situations that were not for the faint of heart. A man of undoubted courage, Bartlett believed in scientific fact. Nonetheless, he admitted to having had enough unusual experiences to make him a believer in the supernatural, even if only a reluctant one. Bartlett had a story of a strange occurrence that took place not in the Arctic, but in his hometown of Brigus.

Bartlett's uncle was captain of a ship called the *Falcon*. One day in 1894, the *Falcon* set sail from Philadelphia, bound for St. John's with a cargo of coal. A few days after the *Falcon*'s departure, Bartlett was sitting in his home in Brigus when a neighbour ran in and made an astonishing announcement. She had just walked past the home of a crew member on board the *Falcon* named Harry Smith, and had seen Harry in the window. Bartlett said that wasn't possible, because Harry was aboard the *Falcon*, which was not due in port for several days. The neighbour insisted that she had seen Harry, and began to wonder if something had happened to him: she had seen a forerunner. Several days later the people of Brigus received bad news. The *Falcon* had gone down with all hands.

The Wreck of the *Ella M. Rudolph*

On December 6, 1926, the schooner *Ella M. Rudolph*, en route from St. John's to Port Nelson, was caught by a blizzard and smashed to pieces on the rocky coast. Captain Eleazer Blackwood and six other people died, including the skipper's sons Bertram and Harry, and his brother-in-law, Samuel Carter. The only survivor was the captain's youngest son, Duke. Miraculously, the youth was thrown ashore and managed to climb up a cliff face to safety. Then he walked five miles to the community of Little Catalina in search of help.

Newfoundlanders have songs memorializing almost every ship that ever sank in Newfoundland waters. The *Ella M. Rudolph* is no exception. The following verses are from a song composed by Hughie Sexton of Trinity in 1926.

On the sixth day of December, the *Rudolph* left the town,
With a general load of cargo, for Port Nelson she was
bound;
At three o'clock that evening, through the Tickle she did
pass,
With a threatening of a violent breeze showing through
the glass.

It was not far out in the bay when the schooner she did
reef,
The skipper he did change his course from the north
unto nor'east;
The schooner scarce had struck a rock, she was covered
by a wave,
And all her crew except one man had met a watery grave.

The vessel barely struck the rocks before covered with
the waves,
All her crew except one man did meet a watery grave;
The poor young lad jumped overboard thro' blinding
snow and drift,
And by the hands of providence got hove into the cliff.

In addition to the song, the sad tale of the *Ella M. Rudolph* has
an accompanying ghost story; or perhaps, rather, an example of a
forerunner. A man named Elias Burry, a lay reader in his church, was
lying on his couch when: "Suddenly my door opened and in walked a
soaking wet Samuel Carter, my good friend." Burry said that the man
was wearing oilskins and holding a lantern. He stood in the middle
of the room for a few seconds, and then departed without uttering a
word. At that very moment, Samuel Carter was drowning amidst the
wreckage of the *Ella M. Rudolph*. His body was one of two that were
never recovered.

"How True!"

Ghosts are mysteries. For all the serious study that has been done on the paranormal, we still don't know exactly what ghosts are, and many people flatly deny that they exist at all. But what about ghosts that, ironically, help to *solve* mysteries? Literature is full of them. Arguably the most famous of them is the ghost of Hamlet's father, who appears to the moody prince and reveals that he was a victim of murder.

There is no shortage of stories about ghosts helping the living to solve crimes, locate treasure, and unravel mysteries. They have even been known to inform people of ships lost at sea. One such Newfoundland story is about a ship called the *Gertrude*.

The *Gertrude*, commanded by Captain Thomas Carew, sailed out of St. John's to pick up sealers who were hunting along the Southern Shore. The ship vanished without a trace, and for a long time her fate was a mystery. One day a man whose brother was one of the *Gertrude's* crewmen was in the woods, hunting. Suddenly he saw a man sitting on a rock. As he drew nearer, a strange feeling came over him. To his disbelief, he realized that the man on the rock was his brother, who was missing, along with the *Gertrude* and her whole company.

With the uncomfortable idea that he must be in the presence of a ghost, the man asked, "Did you make Renews Rock?" (a rock outside Renews Harbour). The ghost replied, "How true, how true!" Then vanished. The wreck of the *Gertrude* was located on the bottom of the sea, not far from Renews Rock.

The Ghosts of HMS *Harpooner*

Major shipwrecks and other maritime disasters, like battles, were often the scenes of large and sudden loss of life. On a stricken vessel, crowded with people, terror reigned as passengers prayed while the mariners fought storms or in-rushing seas. When the fight was over, and the sea had claimed yet another victory, did the souls of all those victims, whose last moments of life were fraught with fear, rest as uneasily as those of soldiers who died

Many Newfoundland ghost stories begin with a shipwreck. This scene is from C. J. Vernet's painting, "Seascape: The Storm".

en masse on battlefields? Apparently, many of the unfortunate souls of those who perished in maritime disasters never found eternal peace.

The mighty *Titanic* sank in 1912 after striking an iceberg about four hundred miles off the coast of Newfoundland, taking over 1500 people to their deaths. A very popular travelling Titanic exhibit, which displays artifacts recovered from the wreck, is said to be haunted by the ghosts of some of those people. In 1914 the *Empress of Ireland* sank after a collision in the St. Lawrence River; over a thousand people died. Divers who have gone down to the wreck have said that they believe it is haunted. In 1915 a German submarine torpedoed the *Lusitania* off the coast of Ireland, sending her to the bottom along with 1,198 people. The wreck is said not only to be haunted, but also cursed. Nineteenth-century sailing ships couldn't carry as many people as one of these great liners, so the loss of life in even a large shipwreck at that time was not comparable. By the standards of the time, however, one disaster that took place off the coast of Newfoundland was of catastrophic proportions. It was bound to result in unquiet souls.

On November 10, 1816, the British transport ship HMS *Harpooner* was wrecked near St. Shott's in St. Mary's Bay. The ship was carrying soldiers and their families home to England. More than two hundred men, women, and children died. According to local tradition, some marines who had managed to get ashore were buried alive when a portion of cliff, weakened by the storm and seas, collapsed on them. The site has since been known as Marine's Cove. In terms of loss of life, the wreck of the *Harpooner* was one of the worst marine calamities in Newfoundland history.

Many years after the disaster, some fishermen who were unfamiliar with the history of the area anchored their boat in Marine's Cove. During the night, the man on watch saw one longboat towing another. Both were full of men, women, and children. A big man was at the helm. As the longboat passed the fishing boat, the helmsman called up to the man on watch, "What's our course to clear Cape English?" The lookout answered, "Nor, Nor-east." The watchman believed he had just seen the survivors of a shipwreck, so he went below to tell the captain. The other crewmen came on deck in time to see the lantern of the longboat disappear toward the shore.

The next morning, with a gale blowing, the fisherman searched the shore for signs of the wreck or other survivors. They found nothing. When they told local residents about the lifeboats full of people, they were told that they had seen the ghosts of the doomed *Harpooner*.

The Keys

The inhabitants of Newfoundland's outport communities were hardy people. But as self-sufficient as they were, they were always willing to lend a hand to a neighbour in need. One such act of selflessness was repaid with a life-saving warning from a man on his deathbed — many miles from the site of a near-tragedy.

The winter of 1863 had been a hard one at St. Mary's. Fishing had been poor, and game scarce. Toward the end of winter, everybody was running out of supplies. On the evening of Ash Wednesday, Con Sullivan was in his house playing cards with some friends, when his neighbour, Mat Cooney, entered and said, "God save all here." Mat had a wife and eight children, and they were out of food. He asked Con for a pan of flour, saying, "I haven't got a crumb left."

Standing up from his card game, Con said, "Well, Mat, b'y, I am on the last barrel of flour, and half of it's yours."

Finally, winter ended and the fishing season began. On May 1 Con and his crew went out to the fishing grounds at Cape St. Mary's. At the mouth of St. Mary's Bay there is a breaker known as the Keys. It was a dangerous place; the cause of many wrecks and lost lives.

Con and his men had been out for three weeks and were returning home with a full load of fish. Just before nightfall, a thick fog rolled in. Visibility was zero. At 2:30 a.m., crewman Tom Fewer came on deck with a mug of tea for the captain. Fewer recalled later, "As I looked, I saw the form of another man standing by the skipper. I could feel the hair rise on the back of my neck. All the crew were in bed, and the Captain was alone on deck. It was a misty form that stood near him. As I looked, I heard a shout: 'The Keys, the Keys! 'ard down, for God's sake! 'ard down!' The skipper acted quickly and spun the wheel. We narrowly escaped hitting the Keys. When I looked at the Captain, the misty figure had disappeared. The Captain turned to me and said, "Well, b'y, I was well-paid for the half-barrel of flour I gave Mat Cooney last Ash Wednesday. He came by me and let a screech out of him: 'The Keys, the Keys! 'ard down, for God's sake, 'ard down!'"

No doubt this must have been perplexing to Tom Fewer. How could Mat Cooney "come by"? He might have thought the captain had taken leave of his senses, had he himself not seen that misty form of a man. But could *that*, whatever it was, have been Mat Cooney? It was all very strange. And, as it turned out, the explanation was just as strange.

When Con and his crew arrived in St. Mary's, they learned that Mat Cooney had died at 2:30 that morning. Just before he expired he stunned the friends and relatives around his bed when he suddenly sat up and shouted, "The Keys! The Keys!" Then he lay back and died.

The Dower Mystery

Another story in which a spirit crosses a vast expanse of water to appear on a ship is that of a captain named Dower and his wife Ellen. It is, in fact, one of Newfoundland's most oft-told ghost stories. One version was even included in the multi-volume *Book of Newfoundland* edited by Joseph R. Smallwood. There are minor differences in some versions. In one, the story tales place in 1873, the captain's name is John, and his ship is the *Eleanor*. In another, the year is 1872, Edward is the captain's name, and he is skipper of the *Elsie*. Part of the story's appeal is that besides being a ghost story, it is a tale of undying love.

On March 10, 1872, Captain Edward Dower and his son set out in the *Eleanor* from their home port of Conche, bound for the sealing grounds. Over the years the Dower family had prospered from the seal hunt, and the skipper anticipated another good season. But he also looked forward to the day when he would return to the arms of his beloved wife Ellen. As the ship cleared harbour for the open sea, Ellen also began counting the days until her dear Ned would come home.

About a week after Captain Dower had sailed, Ellen suddenly fell ill. Her condition worsened in just a matter of hours. She slipped into a coma, and died. The whole community went into mourning. Ellen Dower had been loved and respected by everyone because of her gentle nature and acts of charity. From all over, friends and neighbours came to grieve at her wake. Everyone remarked on the peaceful look on her face as she lay in her coffin. It was as though she were asleep, and the hand of death had not touched her.

According to tradition, there would be a three-day wake for Ellen before her burial. Much to everyone in the community's surprise, the *Eleanor* sailed into the harbor on the night of the second day, well ahead of her expected return. The ship's flag was at half mast, in mourning. What happened at the wake was even more astonishing.

It was customary to always have someone keeping vigil over the deceased, regardless of the hour, until the body was taken to the graveyard. The mourners who were sitting watch over Ellen on the second night were startled when a long sigh suddenly came from the corpse. Then it moved.

Some of the mourners fled in terror. The braver ones remained, and before their very eyes, Ellen sat up in her coffin. She said, "I am tired. I have been far. I have been with Ned." Then she lay back down, and was still.

As far as Captain Dower was concerned, Ellen had indeed been with him. While his ship was out in the ice fields, Ellen's ghost had come to him, carried there by her love for him, her anxiety for him, and her heart at one with his. Believing that he had seen a portent of her death, the captain had turned his ship homeward. He arrived in time to look upon her face one more time before she was put into the ground. Captain Dower never went to the sealing grounds again.

The Wrecker

In the days of wooden sailing ships, "wrecking" was a particularly vile form of piracy. Wreckers would use false beacons to lure ships into dangerous waters. When the ship struck a reef, the crew would have to take to the lifeboat and try to get to shore. Whether or not they made it was of no concern to the wreckers. The villains would then either row out and plunder the abandoned ship, or wait for the surf to pound it to pieces, and then collect the barrels and cases of cargo that came ashore with the tide. Even the timbers of a wrecked ship were valuable, because they could be used in the construction of houses. However, it was said that in a house that was even partially made from pieces of a wrecked ship, the occupants could hear the screams of drowning sailors at night.

In some places, wreckers were called "blackbirds"; in others they were known as "moon cussers," because on moonlit nights they could not practice their evil trade. One Newfoundland ghost story tells of a suspected wrecker whose criminal ways had dramatic supernatural consequences.

About 150 years ago a mysterious Englishman lived in the vicinity of St. Shott's. He behaved in a suspicious manner and usually avoided other people. Local residents referred to him as the Wrecker, because they believed he was involved in that dirty business.

One night the Southern Shore was hit by one of the worst storms it had known in years. Most people stayed indoors. The next morning, after the weather had cleared, local fishermen found debris along the shore: evidence of a shipwreck. Floating amidst the debris was the body of a beautiful young woman. Nearby was the Wrecker himself, stumbling along the shore in a state of shock.

An investigation revealed that the Wrecker had in fact used a lantern to lure a vessel to its destruction. When he went out to plunder the ship, he discovered the body of the girl. He immediately recognized her as the daughter of a woman he had known and loved in England, but who had rejected his marriage proposal. He had sailed to Newfoundland because of a broken heart and, once there, taken up the life of a criminal and recluse.

The cove near St. Shott's where this wreck occurred is now said to be haunted. Just before a storm blows in, the spirit of the dead girl appears on the beach. Kneeling beside her, weeping, is the ghost of the Wrecker.

The Phantom Galley

Tales of ghost ships are common in Newfoundland and Labrador lore. Reports of spectral vessels have included every sort of craft from tall ships of the great age of sail, to Second World War German U-boats. Given the province's rich nautical culture and history, it would be surprising if there *weren't* a few ghost ships looming out in the fog. But what reasonable explanation could account for the sightings of an ancient Greek galley in Newfoundland waters?

The warships and merchant vessels of the ancient Greeks were basically big rowboats with a single sail to help them along. They were made for the Mediterranean and its adjacent seas. Ancient mariners like the Greeks preferred to hug the coastline, and did not sail out of sight of land unless it was absolutely necessary. Their ships were certainly not suited to voyages on the open Atlantic Ocean. Though it would be possible for a Greek galley to make a trans-Atlantic crossing, the odds against one doing so would have been high. Even with a good wind, galleys were slow. And they could not carry the large amounts of food and water needed to sustain the crew for a voyage of many weeks.

Nonetheless, in the 1920s there were reports of a ghostly galley in Placentia Bay. People who claimed to have seen it said that it was manned by a phantom crew that laboured at two banks of oars. The apparition was almost like an ancient Greek version of the legendary *Flying Dutchman.*

What made the phantom Greek galley even more frightening than the *Dutchman* was that it looked like it was on fire! Ship and crew alike were engulfed in flames. Witnesses reportedly said that they could feel the heat, and hear the cries of the men. Then the ship would vanish.

There have been no reports of the phantom galley in almost ninety years. Just what did the people of Placentia Bay see? Was an image from some ancient sea battle somehow transported through time and space? Why was the apparition ablaze? We know that the ancient Greeks, who were constantly at war with each other, had a weapon called Greek Fire. Using a device that was something like a modern day flame thrower, the Greeks would launch streams of fire at enemy ships, with devastating results. Perhaps the phantom galley was an inexplicable glimpse at the last moments of a ship and crew as they perished in a sea battle, long, long ago and far away.

The Ghost Light of Trinity

Almost a century after the newspaper report about the lights on the Gulf of St. Lawrence, the people of Trinity began seeing a strange light on the water. The mysterious light appeared nightly and for such a long period of time, that it became something of a tourist attraction. People came from other parts of Newfoundland just to see the Trinity Light.

The phenomenon began one night in 1916, when a bright light was seen a few miles from the Narrows at Trinity. At first people paid it little attention, because they took it for the light of an incoming ship. The Fort Point Lighthouse keeper thought it was a vessel called the *Prospero* coming into port. He got into his boat and rowed across the harbour to the public wharf to be on hand when she docked. But while the light keeper and a few others stood on the dock, watching and waiting, the light suddenly disappeared.

There was some concern in the community. This was during the First World War, and people were afraid that the light might have come from a German submarine. Perhaps the enemy intended to cut the vital Transatlantic Cable, or even shell the town! Such fears were not as outlandish as it might seem today. Submarines were a new and little understood weapon, as far as civilians were concerned. Considering the damage they were doing to Allied shipping, it is little wonder that people in coastal communities lived in fear of submarine raids.

Every night for the next week the mysterious light appeared, always between the hours of 9 and 11 p.m. Hundreds of people would gather at the wharf to watch. Although the appearance of the light was never accompanied by any sign of German naval action, the people of Trinity were worried. They finally reported their concerns to the government in St. John's and the Heart's Content Cable Company. They were told that nobody was trying to sabotage the Transatlantic Cable, and that it was unlikely any German submarines were lurking in the waters off Trinity Bay. This reassured the nervous population, but it did not explain the strange light.

One night a group of fishermen bravely set out in a boat to investigate the light themselves. As they drew near, the light vanished. Some old timers believed it was the spectre of a ship that had gone down with all hands.

The light continued to appear after the Armistice of November 11, 1918, ending once and for all any speculation that it might be a skulking German submarine. The light continued to hold the community's fascination, though. On December 24, 1925, it was the subject of a letter to the editor that appeared in the St. John's *Evening Telegram*. The author of the letter, Mr. W. White of Trinity, invited the citizens of St. John's to come out and see the light for themselves. Then in 1928 the ghostly light abruptly ceased to appear. It has not been seen since, and it has never been satisfactorily explained.

Ghosts on the Ice

For many years the annual seal hunt on the ice fields off the shores of Newfoundland has been a focal point of international controversy. Whatever side one takes in this very complex issue, there is no reasonable argument against the fact that in the old days of the seal hunt, going out on the ice to get the "swiles" (seals) was one of the most dangerous jobs in the world. Living under appalling shipboard conditions, men trekked across the heaving ice floes, many miles from land, hoping to bring in enough seal pelts to help pay down the ever-present debts they owed to the merchants in their home ports. Newfoundland sealers died by the score on the ice fields from drowning and other accidents, and when their ships were crushed by the ice and went down.

Because "swiling" called for stamina and courage, it became a traditional rite of passage. Young Newfoundlanders went to the hunting grounds (also called the Front) for the first time as boys and returned home as men. As one old fisherman in St. Anthony told visiting Toronto journalist Val Clery in an undated interview, "In those days you weren't thought much of a man if you didn't go swiling." The fisherman, whose name Clery did not record, said that he had lost his father in the Sealing Disaster of 1914.

On March 31 of that year, 132 men from the ship *Newfoundland* went onto the ice in search of the main seal herd. The *Newfoundland* was commanded by Westbury Kean, son of Captain Abraham Kean, who commanded another ship called the *Stephano*. Captain Abe, as he was known, was the most successful sealing captain in Newfoundland history, bringing in more than a million pelts in his long career. But he was also known as a hard taskmaster who did not believe in pampering his men. He had no use for new-fangled gadgets, like ship radios.

The men from the *Newfoundland* crossed six miles of ice to Captain Abe's ship, where they had expected to spend the night. Instead, Captain Abe sent them back over the ice and told them to return to their own ship. A severe storm blew in, catching the men out on the open ice. Due to their lack of communication devices, Wes Keane and Captain Abe each thought the men were on the other ship.

The stranded men endured two horrific days of frigid temperatures and murderous winds. By the time rescuers found them, seventy-seven men had frozen to death or drowned. The survivors were barely clinging to life. Five of the bodies had disappeared beneath the ice and were never recovered. Many Newfoundlanders held Captain Abe responsible for the tragedy, but his strong political connections in St. John's protected him from accountability.

The fisherman told Clery that he was only five years old when his father died under Captain Abe's command. About ten years later, he himself went swiling and his captain was also Abraham Kean.

True to his reputation as Newfoundland's greatest sealer, Captain Abe quickly found the main herd. "Go to it, me sons," he cried, as the men went over the side.

"It was hard going," the fisherman said. "The wind'd cut through you, and the ice pans was buckling and shifting … the watch master yelled out to me, 'Mind you stay close by me, boy; there'll be snow before night. And your mother'd never forgive me if I lost you.'"

During the hunt, a storm blew in and the fisherman got separated from the rest of the men. Driving snow reduced visibility to zero, and soon he was utterly lost. "I was terrible afraid, terrible afraid," he said. "All alone there in the snow with night coming on."

He stumbled across the ice until he came to a ten-foot-high pressure ridge. He hadn't the strength to climb over it, so he used his gaff to dig out a tiny cave, and then crawled inside. Shivering so badly that his teeth were chattering, he was certain he would die. He tried to fight off sleep, as he had heard that if you fell asleep out there in the cold, you never woke up. He didn't know how long he lay curled up in that hole, but after some time he opened his eyes and saw that night had fallen, and it had stopped snowing. "Then," the fisherman told Clery, "I noticed something strange."

Five whitecoats lay on the ice just a few feet from him. He'd heard of hungry men on the ice eating seal pup hearts raw. He had also heard of them burning seal pup fat to keep warm. He decided he would try to kill one of the whiteheads with his gaff.

Too weak to walk, he crawled toward the pups, certain they would be frightened away at any moment. Just as he reached them, the nearest whitehead looked at him, and to the boy's amazement it had his father's face! He knew that face well, he said, because he had often gazed at his father's photograph at home. To his further astonishment, he heard his father's voice softly say, "So you came out on the ice, me son, like your dad. You should've had more sense."

The voice stopped him from killing the pups. "No, son, no. You can't kill them as is dead already. Don't be afraid. We'll save you and look after you out here. In the long run, Abram Kean'll come back and find you. Black as his heart is, he'd not dare to leave both father and son to die out here on the ice."

As the boy lay on the ice, the whiteheads all pressed themselves against him and warmed him with their body heat. "There, son, that'll keep the life in you." The voice continued to explain that the souls of men who died on the ice went into whitecoats, and remained there "until their time came to go to their rest." The souls of the boy's father and the four men who had died with him — the sealers whose bodies hadn't been recovered after the 1914 disaster — were now awaiting Captain Abe. "We'll not rest till the man as left us out here to die, dies himself and faces up to us."

The boy fell asleep. When he awoke to the sound of a ship's whistle, it was daylight. Captain Abe's ship was just a few hundred yards away, moving toward him through the ice. The seal pups were still there, but, "They looked like ordinary swiles now." He thought he must have dreamed the whole thing, but one of the pups raised its head and spoke again in his father's voice. "You mind to tell Abraham Keane, me son, we's waiting for him out here whenever his time comes."

As the boy approached the ship, two men came down to the ice to help him. They were amazed that he was still alive: he'd been missing for *three days*! When he came aboard the ship, he found Captain Abe in a rage. "So you go and get yourself lost, boy, first time out on the ice," Kean roared. "And you lose us nigh on half a day's swiling looking for you. How you're alive is still a mystery to me. The good Lord must've taken pity on you, which is more'n I'd be willing to do."

Captain Abe looked at the five seal pups on the ice, and told the boy, "I'll tell you what you're going to do now, boy. You're going to get back

The deck of a ship is piled with the bodies of men who died in the Sealing Disaster of 1914. Sailors reported seeing the ghosts of the victims out on the ice.

on that ice and you're going to sculp [skin] them five whitecoats you left lying out there, so's we can see if there's the making of a man in you at all. Now go to it!"

The boy refused, saying that the pups had kept him alive. Then he said, "Cap'n Kean, I've a message for you. When I was out on that ice, I saw me father. And he told me to tell you that he and the four other men you left to die out there'd be waiting for you when your time comes."

Kean told the watch master that the boy was obviously weak in the head and to take him below. He also ordered him to send some men over the side to sculp the seals. The watch master replied, "You heard what the boy said, Cap'n. No man of mine is going to kill them swiles. You had us killing swiles the three days since this boy was lost and you never gave a second thought to finding him till we came on him by accident. You're lucky you don't have the death of father and son on your conscience — if you have a conscience."

Abraham Kean died in 1945. The old fisherman told Clery that after that first near-fatal trip to the Front, he never went swiling again. He also said, "But if only I could be certain Abram Kean's soul was out there in one of them whitecoats, I'd be out there killing swiles now."

Val Clery's narrator was not the only person in Newfoundland to report a strange experience in connection with the 1914 Sealing Disaster. Canadian folklorist Edith Fowke recorded a story told by Pat Maher of Pouch Cove. The tale is rooted in the belief that on the anniversary of their death, ghosts will return to the place where they died.

Following the 1914 disaster, the *Newfoundland* did not participate in the seal hunt again until 1916 after undergoing extensive refitting. She was also renamed the *San Blandford* and Pat Maher was one of the crew. At the end of March, the *San Blandford* was in the same vicinity as another sealing ship, the *Terra Nova*. During the night, a thick fog lay upon the ice fields. Suddenly, the *Terra Nova* started blowing her whistle — the signal that there were people out on the ice.

The captain of the *San Blandford* heard the signal and began to blow his ship's whistle, as well, thinking the *Terra Nova* had men on the ice. However, the *Terra Nova's* skipper thought that the men on the ice belonged to the *San Blandford*. Finally, at about ten o'clock that night, the *Terra Nova* stopped sounding her whistle. Assuming that the other ship had her men safely aboard, the captain of the *San Blandford* also stopped signaling.

The next morning, Pat Maher and several crewmen went over to the *Terra Nova*. They were surprised to be asked what time their men finally got aboard the night before: the men out on the ice weren't from the *San Blandford*. But the *Terra Nova* crewmen insisted. "Yes, ye had got men on the ice, because we saw the men. We heard them first hallo and sing out, and we watched them until they walked up the side of the ship and went in the boat."

Maher and the others didn't know what to make of it at first. But some of those crewmen who had seen the men on the ice climb aboard the *San Blandford* later claimed that they had recognized a few of them as men who had died in the disaster of 1914. The *San Blandford*, after all, was just the old *Newfoundland* with a different name. Her lost men had apparently returned home.

Yet another strange story associated with the Sealing Disaster of 1914 is that of the Crewe family of Trinity Bay. According to this account, Reuben Crewe nearly lost his life in 1911 when the sealing ship he was on sank. After his brush with death, Reuben told his wife Mary that he was through with sealing. The risk just wasn't worth the small financial reward. Mary was pleased to hear this. Far too many women in Newfoundland's ports had lost husbands, fathers, sons, and brothers to the dangers of the seal hunt.

But in March of 1914, Mary Crewe's sixteen-year-old son Albert John proudly announced that he'd obtained a berth on the *Newfoundland*. The boy wanted to go swiling so badly that nothing Mary or Reuben said could change his mind. Finally, Reuben signed onto the *Newfoundland*, too: he might not be able to stop his son from going to the Front, but he could ship out with the boy and keep an eye on him. As the *Newfoundland* sailed off for the ice, Mary Crewe could only pray that she would see her husband and son again.

She did, but not in the way she would have wished. Mary went to bed one night, thinking about Reuben and Albert John working out there on the hazardous ice. She awoke suddenly and saw Reuben and Albert John kneeling beside her bed. Their heads were bowed in prayer, and there was an air of calm about them. This forerunner, for that's probably what it was, left Mary with a feeling of dread.

Not long after, Mary Crewe learned of the disaster. Reuben and Albert John were among the dead. Their bodies had been found in an embrace, as though they had been trying to keep each other warm. Their faces were frozen forever in a look of peace, just as Mary Crewe had seen them when they paid her a final visit.

X Marks the Spot

Guardians of Pirate Treasure

Many years ago, when I was enrolled at the University of Waterloo in Ontario, I had the good fortune to meet Harold Horwood. Harold was a well known Newfoundland writer and historian. He had come to the University of Waterloo as writer-in-residence. I was a member of a writers' group in the Department of Integrated Studies, so naturally I invited Harold to come to one of our meetings.

Harold and I became friends and ended up collaborating on a book about Canadian outlaws. He had done considerable research on the pirates who had once prowled the waters off Newfoundland and the Maritimes Provinces, which perfectly complemented my own research on Canadian outlaws. Through Harold's chapters I became familiar with such fascinating characters as the pirates Peter Easton and Eric Cobham.

Easton built a pirate fort at Harbour Grace in 1611 and used it as a base to raid the Spanish Main. He and his pirates fought a battle with the Basques at Harbour Grace; the pirates who were killed in the fight were buried nearby, in a place that is still called the Pirates' Graveyard. It is the only known pirate burial ground in North America, and I would not be at all surprised to hear that it is haunted. Easton was one of the most successful pirates who ever lived, and retired an extremely wealthy man.

Eric Cobham lived about a century after Easton. His principal partner in crime was Maria Lindsey, who was notorious for her cruelty. Using Bay St. George as a base, Cobham hijacked fur ships coming

A battle at Peter Easton's pirate fort at Harbour Grace. The slain pirates were buried at a nearby site that is still called the Pirates' Graveyard. It is the only known burial site of its kind in North America.

down from Quebec. The furs were then sold at great profit on the black market. Cobham was never caught. He got away with his robberies because he didn't leave witnesses: he murdered the crews and sank the captured ships once they'd been looted. The ship owners would assume the missing vessel had been lost in a storm. Cobham eventually retired to a life of luxury in France; Maria Lindsey went insane and committed suicide by leaping off a cliff into the sea. In other versions of the story, she was actually pushed by Cobham. Toward the end of his life, Cobham confessed to his crimes and arranged to have his life story published posthumously. His family attempted to suppress the book, but a copy eventually found its way into the French archives.

We are all familiar with stories of buried pirate treasure. Supposedly, any pirate worth his salt left at least one chest of gold doubloons buried in the sand somewhere. The pirates of legend, Captain Kidd, Blackbeard, Bartholomew Roberts, and Edward Low, were all said to have taken the secret locations of hoarded loot to their graves. In many of the tales, the pirate captain kills a member of his crew and buries the body with the treasure, so that the dead pirate's ghost will guard it.

While some pirates may have stashed gold and silver away in hidden places, most of these stories are based on myth. In fact, it is largely the invention of novelists like Robert Louis Stevenson, author of the classic *Treasure Island*. Pirates generally squandered their ill-gotten gains on rum, women, and gambling. They lived for the moment with little thought for tomorrow, especially since tomorrow might bring death in battle or on the gallows.

But legends, like the pirates themselves, die hard: treasure hunters are still searching for the plunder of Captain Kidd and his pirate brethren. And then there's the story of Shellbird Island in the Humber River, near Corner Brook. Shellbird Island, which lies below a natural rock formation resembling a human face, is a legendary site of buried pirate treasure. And both Peter Easton and Eric Cobham are historically associated with the island.

The Cobham connection is based on the story that nearby Sandy Point was his principal lair. However, there have been other, more compelling arguments that the treasure, if it is there at all, was left by Peter Easton. According to these accounts, Easton didn't confine his pirate raids to the Spanish Main but also hit the fur-bearing ships coming from Quebec. During one of his raids, Easton was forced to withdraw due to the sudden appearance of a French warship.

Deeming discretion the better part of valour, and hoping to evade capture, Easton sailed to the mouth of the Humber River to hide. Legend has it that Easton sent his first mate and a sailor to Shellbird Island with three treasure chests. The men buried them in three different spots. At the third location, as the sailor was about to fill in the hole, the first mate killed him, and dumped the corpse into the pit, thus providing the required ghost to do duty as a sentinel. However, bad luck befell the first mate. At the Devil's Dancing Pool on the Humber River his boat overturned and he was drowned. Easton didn't know the exact location of the treasure sites. He searched for them, but never found them.

For centuries the treasures lay undiscovered. Then, according to one story, late in the nineteenth century some lucky fortune hunters found one of the chests and secretly divided up the loot. In 1934 it was rumoured that the second chest had been found. Again, the riches in it were secretly shared among the fortunate few.

When Harold Horwood and I were collaborating on our book, he didn't mention anything about the treasure and ghost stories to me. Perhaps he wanted to stick to what he considered the cold, hard facts. Nonetheless, I was thrilled to come across this legend connected to Peter Easton. Maybe the third treasure chest still lies hidden, guarded by the ghost of the murdered pirate. The Shellbird Island story is but one of many swashbuckling Newfoundland and Labrador tales of blood, buried treasure, and ghosts.

Torbay's Treasure Cove

In the first quarter of the eighteenth century, the period known as the Golden Age of Piracy, many freebooters were drawn to the coast of Newfoundland. Its hidden coves were excellent places in which they could repair and careen their ships, and stock up on food and fresh water. They could also recruit men — both willing and unwilling — from the fishing stations. If there is truth to the legends, these coves were perfect spots in which to stash away plunder. Treasure Cove on the north side of Torbay Harbour, a few miles north of St. John's, is one such location.

According to a very old story, an unnamed pirate captain sailed into Torbay after a successful summer of raiding the Spanish Main. He decided that the isolated cove would be a perfect place to deposit some of his stolen gold, silver, and jewellery. He called on his crew for volunteers to go ashore with him to help bury the loot and mark the site. The crewmen were veteran pirates, and they knew that anyone who went off with the captain was not likely to come back. However, there was a boy on board who had been taken off a captured ship and pressed into service as a cabin boy. This lad, perhaps thinking he would get into the captain's good graces, volunteered. Maybe the captain would even remove the fetters from his hands and feet. None of the pirates dared to warn him of the danger.

When the captain and the boy prepared to set off in the ship's boat with a chest full of riches, another passenger joined them: a big Newfoundland dog that was the ship's mascot. During his captivity the boy had befriended the dog. As the ship's boat was about to shove off, the dog jumped into it. Considering the dog to be his obedient beast, the captain was unconcerned.

Somewhere in the woods near the shore of Treasure Cove, the obliging cabin boy helped the captain dig a deep hole while the dog sat watching. The unsuspecting youngster had just assisted the captain in lowering the treasure chest into the pit, when the pirate suddenly drew his cutlass and, in one slash, decapitated him. The body and the head dropped into the hole, coating the chest with blood.

The enraged Newfoundland dog snarled, bared its teeth, and leapt at the captain. Even though the pirate was startled, he was too fast for the dog. Another slash with the cutlass, and the big dog was dead. The captain tossed its body into the hole along with the murdered boy. He filled in the hole and returned to his ship.

The villainous captain never came back to pick up his buried loot, though. He might have been killed in battle, drowned in a storm, or hanged on a gallows. The secret of his treasure died with him. The burial site was just another lonely spot on a wild coastline.

That is until, one night many years later, two Torbay fishermen landed on the beach at Treasure Cove. They had heard the beach was haunted and were unnerved by it. But the weather was bad, and they had a boatload of fish.

The fishermen had barely set foot on dry land when a big Newfoundland dog came bounding out of the woods toward them. At first they thought that it must belong to a local family. But as it drew nearer, they could see that its eyes glowed with a hellish red fire. Then behind it, with chains rattling on hands and feet, came the headless ghost of the cabin boy.

The terrified fishermen put their backs to the dory, and in spite of the dark and the foul weather, they pushed off and manned the oars. The horrible apparitions pursued them as far as the water's edge. The men made it home safely, but because they had seen the headless ghost and the phantom dog, they were cursed. One of them soon suffered an accident that made him an invalid him for the rest of his life, and the other one died within the year.

The Ghosts of Shoal Bay

About 250 years ago, a pirate captain was cruising off the southeast coast of Newfoundland hoping to waylay an unsuspecting merchant vessel bound for St. John's. In his hold was the loot from earlier captures. To the captain's horror, the ship that suddenly hove into view was not a defenseless merchantman, but a British man-o-war. No pirate ever chose to shoot it out with the Royal Navy if there was a chance to escape. With the warship bearing down on him, the pirate captain turned toward shore, seeking shallow waters where the larger ship could not follow.

This was not the pirates' lucky day. They ran aground on the deadly shoal at the entrance of the appropriately named Shoal Bay. Hung up on the rock, the pirate ship would be a sitting duck for the guns of the British warship.

The pirate captain ordered his men to bring the treasure up from below and load it into the ship's boat. While they were doing that, he lit a slow burning fuse on a barrel of gunpowder in the magazine. Then he, the first mate, and four crewmen got into the boat and shoved off. No doubt the captain had told the rest of the crew he would be back for them once the treasure was safely ashore. Just as the longboat touched land, the barrel exploded, destroying the vessel and killing every man still on board.

The treasure that the six remaining pirates hauled ashore at Shoal Bay was bound in fourteen packages of gold, silver, and jewels. Each package was so heavy, one man could barely carry it. Once the captain had chosen a site, the four crewmen dug a hole. When it was deep enough, the captain and the first mate lowered the heavy packages to the crewmen waiting at the bottom. When the packages were laid side-by-side at the bottom of the pit, the four men looked up for assistance in climbing out. Instead, they met slashing cold steel. The captain and mate had drawn their cutlasses, and in a swirl of bloody violence, cut the heads off all four crewmen. Now only two people knew where the treasure was, and they had four dead men to guard it.

The captain and the mate filled in the hole and erased all signs of digging. Then they made a map. This map showed the general location of the site, but not the exact spot where the fourteen packages of loot lay buried. That vital bit of information was known only to the captain and the mate. They intended to come back for the swag as soon as they had the means of getting it out of Newfoundland.

The two murderers set off for St. John's, about ten miles to the north. Bad luck still dogged them. A storm blew in, and they became lost. They wandered in the woods for days before the mate died from exposure. The captain finally staggered into Holyrood on Conception Bay. He was cold, starving, and almost dead. One of the villagers took the stranger in and tried to nurse him back to health, but it was too late.

As the captain lay on his death bed, he told the good Samaritan about the treasure, and gave him the map. The Holyrood man dismissed the pirate's story as delirious ranting. When the captain died, he gave him a Christian burial, and put the so-called treasure map away in his sea chest.

The Holyrood man eventually left Newfoundland and moved to the United States. Over the years he forgot all about the treasure map tucked away in his sea chest. Only when he was a grandfather did he rediscover it. He showed it to his grandson as he spun fanciful tales of a dying pirate and buried treasure.

When the man died, the map was passed on to his grandson. Now a grown man, he thought that the map might actually be a key to buried treasure. He went to Newfoundland, and found work in the fishery with a Petty Harbour planter. He didn't want anyone to know that he was searching for treasure, but after a few unsuccessful expeditions to Shoal Bay, he realized that he would need local help.

The young American befriended a St. John's fisherman named Michael Monahan. He told Monahan his grandfather's story, and showed him the map. Monahan was well aware of local legends about pirate gold, and believed that the old map was authentic. When the fishing season was over in the autumn, he said, they could get a few adventurous young lads together and go after the Shoal Bay treasure.

The American agreed, but wicked fate struck again. The very next day he suffered a fatal accident: he drowned when he fell through the hatchway of a fish stage! Monahan was saddened by the sudden death of his new friend, but lost no time gaining possession of the map.

When the fishing season was over, Monahan and three friends went to Shoal Bay to search for the treasure. They set up camp, expecting to be there for at least a few days. The very first night, at the stroke of midnight, they were awakened by ghostly voices all around the camp. Monahan crawled out of the tent to see what was going on, but his three friends huddled inside in terror.

Monahan stoked up the campfire and kept it going all night. In the morning, when his friends finally came out of the tent, Monahan told them that ghosts of the dead pirates had come out of the darkness, but the firelight had forced them to stay back. He said they had watched him until they finally disappeared with the light of dawn.

The four young men had had enough of Shoal Bay. They packed up their gear and left, never to return. However, they carried the curse of the pirate treasure with them. Before the year was out, all of them died under mysterious circumstances. What became of the map is not known.

For many years after the Monahan expedition, nobody tried to find the Shoal Bay treasure. Then, in about 1900, a St. John's man named John Doyle heard the story. He and some friends had planned a fishing trip to Shoal Bay, and decided it would be fun to do a little treasure hunting, too. They set up camp, and after a pleasant evening by the campfire, they retired to their tent.

One of the men had brought along his small dog. It was curled up next to him, sleeping on the tent's dirt floor. At midnight the men were awakened when the dog suddenly began to bark and whine. It trembled with fear, and dug furiously in the ground. Doyle went to the door of the tent, thinking there might be a bear or wolf prowling around. What he saw caused him to gasp out loud, bringing his friends to the tent door.

It was a dark, moonless night, but out on the water they could see the strange glow of a ghostly, eighteenth-century sailing ship. Fluttering from the mainmast was the Jolly Roger; the black flag of piracy. As the men looked on, unable to believe their eyes, a longboat was lowered over the ship's side. Six men got into it and began to row for shore. Just as the boat reached the beach, near the very spot where Doyle and his party were camped, the pirate ship suddenly and silently exploded in a mass of flames. For a moment the light lit up the entire bay. Then the ship and the longboat were gone — but that wasn't the end of the night's horrors.

Still transfixed, the men watched a sinister-looking black form slither out of the water and up the beach toward them. The dog yelped and whimpered. The men were hypnotized, unable to move. Then the youngest of them, a youth of sixteen, suddenly shouted in terror. He pulled out his camp knife and slashed open the back wall of the tent. This seemed to break whatever spell had held the others. They all fled through that opening, followed by the dog.

The men ran until they reached a barn, where they stayed for the rest of the night. In the morning they returned to their camp. Everything seemed quiet, but they decided there were other places to fish besides Shoal Bay. They packed up their gear and left, abandoning their hopes of finding buried treasure. The Shoal Bay treasure still lies hidden with the bones of the four murdered pirates.

The Ghosts of Copper Island

Next to Peter Easton, the most famous pirate in Newfoundland history was Sir Henry Mainwarring. He was an aristocrat and a master seaman who was sent to Newfoundland by the Crown to apprehend Easton and take him back to England in chains. When Mainwarring arrived in Newfoundland, Easton had vanished. Disappointed that he wouldn't be able to seize Easton's rich plunder, Mainwarring decided to turn pirate himself and use Newfoundland as his base of operations.

In Notre Dame Bay there is a small isle called Copper Island. It was named when, late in the nineteenth century, a fisherman discovered a hoard of old copper coins there. According to legend, one of the ships in Mainwarring's pirate fleet was wrecked nearby; the captain of the vessel salvaged the treasure in his hold and buried it on the island. People believed that the stash of copper coins was but a small part of the pirate hoard, which was protected by ghostly guardians. Local fishermen usually stayed well away from Copper Island.

However, scary stories were not enough to deter all of the treasure hunters. One day a stranger arrived in the community of Musgrave Harbour, about six miles from Copper Island. He said he was going to find the treasure. He purchased a tent and supplies, hired a boat, and set off for Copper Island.

Several weeks passed, and the stranger did not return. A few local men put aside their fear of the haunted place, and went to look for him. They found his boat on the beach, as well as his camp, well-stocked with supplies, the tent still standing. But there was no sign of the stranger. The men spread out to search the island.

They found him in a pit he had been digging just above the high tide mark on the far side of the island. He was dead, his pick and shovel lying at his side. The corpse bore no signs of violence, but his face was the picture of pure terror. The dead eyes were wide open and bulged from their sockets, as though the last thing they had seen was an object of horror. The searchers concluded that the stranger had died of fright. The ghostly guardians had done their grim duty.

For a long time after that no one ventured out to haunted Copper Island. But eventually a band of treasure hunters found the nerve to go after the pirate loot. Like the unfortunate stranger, this group of young men took a tent, picks and shovels, and enough food for several weeks. When they reached Copper Island, they unwittingly set up camp near the very spot where the stranger had died. Then they began to dig.

No sooner had the treasure hunters' picks cut into the earth than something extraordinary happened. A tall-masted, square-rigged, old-time sailing ship suddenly appeared out on the water. From the jackstaff flew the ominous black flag of piracy!

The treasure hunters watched, paralyzed by fear, as the ship from a bygone era sailed straight toward them. She slowed to a drift, and they heard the rattle of an anchor chain unwinding. The ship stopped, and moments later a longboat appeared. The men in it were the most vile-looking seadogs imaginable.

At the sight of these phantom pirates, the treasure hunters dropped their tools and bolted. They ran clear across the island to their boat, jumped in, and rowed like madmen for Musgrave Harbour. That was the last time anyone dared to defy the ghosts of Copper Island. Sir Henry Mainwarring's treasure lies untouched.

The Ghosts of Kelly's Island

> We sailed on, we sailed on, till she came in shot,
> But still this brave pirate, he dreaded us not;
> With voice loud as thunder bold Kelly did say,
> "Fire a shot, strike 'er midships, brave boys, fire away!"
> And it's oh, Britons stand true,
> Stand to your colours, stand true
>
> We fought them in battle for an hour or more,
> Till blood through her scuppers like water did pour;
> With balls of good metal we peppered her hull,
> Till down came her ensign, staff colours and all.
> And it's oh, Britons stand true,
> Stand to your colours, stand true.

These two verses are from a traditional folk ballad called "Kelly the Pirate." It tells the story of a sea fight between a Royal Navy vessel and a pirate ship commanded by a notorious freebooter named Alphonsus Kelly. In the early seventeenth century, Kelly prowled the waters of Newfoundland preying on merchant vessels and pillaging the fishing fleets of equipment and supplies. According to the stories, Kelly was an Irishman, a red bearded giant who was ferocious in battle and struck fear in all who met him. If a member of his own crew dared to challenge his command, Kelly would break the trouble maker's back over his knee and toss him to the sharks. Whenever Kelly captured a ship, he took only one man or boy prisoner. This unfortunate would be murdered and then dumped in a hole with a chest full of treasure.

Kelly's base was an island in Conception Bay that has since been named after him. It covers only five acres and is uninhabited, but Kelly's Island is said to be the hiding place for his loot, including the gold and silver he seized from treasure ships in the Spanish Main. He allegedly also had a fort on the island. The discovery of an old anchor there is considered hard evidence that pirates had used the island to careen their ships. A huge granite boulder once perched precariously on a cliff above a lagoon that cut into the island's shore. This rock was a signpost to the treasure sites. Unfortunately for fortune hunters, it fell into the sea long ago.

Alphonsus Kelly was killed in the battle with the Royal Navy. The surviving members of his crew were taken to England where they were tried and hanged. No living soul knew the exact location of Kelly's treasure, but everyone acquainted with the story knew that the ghosts of Kelly's victims kept guard over the gold and silver.

Amazingly enough, there are three stories about treasure hunters disregarding superstition and going after the loot. In the middle of the nineteenth century, a Newfoundland fishing captain came into possession of a map that showed the location of a treasure site on Kelly's Island, and found some old gold coins. In 1901, a stranger asked a local fisherman to take him out to the island. The fisherman waited in the boat while the stranger went ashore. When the stranger returned, he was carrying an old ship's boiler. People later said that the boiler probably contained loot that the stranger didn't want the fisherman to see. Then, in the 1930s, another stranger supposedly found some old coins on the island.

But even if these stories are true, they account for only a small percentage of the treasure that Kelly the pirate supposedly buried on his island. The bulk of the gold and silver is still there. And so, says local legend, are the ghosts of Kelly's victims.

The Ghosts of Chapel Cove Pond

Tales of treasure and ghosts at Chapel Cove, on the east side of Holyrood Bay, go back to the early eighteenth century, when the area was first settled. Legend says that some local men found a stranger, an old sailor, near death beside Chapel Cove Pond. The dying man told them that pirate treasure was buried nearby. With his final breath he warned them of a terrible curse that would fall upon anyone who tried to get their hands on it.

The men buried the stranger and then, foolishly ignoring the warning, they began to dig for the treasure. They found a strongbox, but were struck dead before they could lift it out of the hole. Presumably, whatever dark force was protecting the treasure covered it up again.

Over the years, other fortune hunters searched for the hidden riches. They always gave up the quest abruptly, and wouldn't say why. Stories circulated about ghost ships and headless phantom pirates.

One Chapel Cove man decided that he would be safe from malignant spirits if he first armoured himself with the protection of the Church. He went to his parish priest and received a blessing that the good father said would ward off evil. In return, the man promised to give the priest a portion of the treasure, for the benefit of the parish's widows and orphans.

The treasure hunter's partner was an old Irishman who was well versed in supernatural lore, and supposedly knew how to deal with spirits. To keep their work secret, they waited for a moonless night, put some picks and shovels in a cart, and set out for Chapel Cove Pond.

As they made their way along the shore of the pond, they suddenly saw a strange light out on the water. Before their disbelieving eyes, the light took the shape of an old sailing ship. Most unnerving of all, the phantom ship was moving along with them as they followed the shoreline.

The sight of the ghost ship greatly frightened the old Irishman. He didn't want to go on. But his partner had faith in the protective blessing he'd received from the priest, and persuaded the nervous old fellow to continue.

They reached their destination at the head of the pond, the place where the dying old sailor had been found years earlier. They hauled their tools out of the cart and began to dig, casting frequent, jittery glances over their shoulders at the ghost ship, which now sat motionless and silent on the water.

The treasure hunter and the Irishman had to dig deep before, at last, they heard the clang of a pick striking an iron box. In their excitement over the prospect of wealth right at their fingertips, they momentarily forgot about the treasure's guardians. They frantically dug away the earth from around the box, and with great exertion pulled it out of the hole.

The two giddy men prepared to lift the heavy box onto the cart. Only then did they suddenly realize that they were not alone. Standing just a few feet away from them was a figure that made their hair stand on end.

The apparition was a huge man with a big red beard, wearing the unmistakable clothing of a sixteenth-century pirate captain. Behind this fearsome figure were two more apparitions: headless pirates with cutlasses in their hands.

The poor, old Irishman, no expert on spirits after all, fainted and fell into the cart. The treasure hunter from Chapel Cove was made of sterner stuff, and besides, he had that protective blessing. No mere fiend from hell was going to stand between him and his dream of fabulous wealth. With a defiant glare at the ghosts, he heaved with all his strength to lift the treasure chest onto the cart. He would take the gold and the unconscious Irishman home, and the ghosts could go back to whatever netherworld they had come from.

But defying dark powers isn't that easy. The red-bearded ghost pirate lashed out and struck the man down with a single blow. While the man was helpless on the ground, the headless ghost pirates came at him with their cutlasses raised. It seemed as though the man was about to lose his own head, but he did not cringe or cower.

With the swords poised to behead him, the man cried out that he had the blessing of the Church. He said he had promised to give a share of the treasure to a priest to help the needy. What use was the gold, he demanded to know, to men who were already dead!

The red-bearded giant then let out such a howl of rage that the man fainted from pure fright. When he regained consciousness, he was lying in the cart next to the Irishman. The blessing had apparently protected his life, but it had not guaranteed that he would get the gold. He looked out at the water, and saw the red-bearded pirate and his headless accomplices returning to their ship in a longboat. They had the treasure chest with them. When they boarded the ship, it disappeared in a wink. The man fell on his knees and gave thanks that he was still alive. He swore on the spot that his treasure hunting days were over.

The Treasures of Captain Kidd

In the seventeenth and eighteenth centuries, some of the most notorious pirates in the annals of the sea visited Newfoundland's shores, including Bartholomew "Black Bart" Roberts and bloodthirsty Edward Low. If there is truth to any of the legends, the man whose name practically became synonymous with the word *pirate*; William Kidd, also came to Newfoundland. Furthermore, say the legends, he left treasure there.

In reality, William Kidd wasn't much of a pirate. He was a respected, middle-aged English sea captain who, in 1695, was commissioned by the Crown to hunt down pirates and attack any ships sailing for France,

The notorious Captain Kidd looks on as his men bury a treasure chest in this 1894 illustration by Howard Pyle. According to legend, pirate captains buried dead men with their treasure, so their ghosts would guard it.

England's principal enemy. For two years Kidd roamed the Atlantic and Indian Oceans, and the Red Sea, in his ship the *Adventure Galley*. He did not capture a single prize.

Pressured by a mutinous crew, Kidd seized four merchant vessels, which he claimed were sailing under the French flag, and sold their cargoes ashore. This only whetted his men's appetite for more plunder. Their next prize was the one that would make Kidd's name as a pirate.

In January 1698, Kidd captured the *Quedah Merchant*, an Indian ship that Kidd claimed was sailing under French authority. This ship was the kind of prize every pirate dreamed of: she was loaded with gold, silver, jewels, and silk — enough loot to make every man aboard the *Adventure Galley* rich.

Unfortunately for Kidd, word of his exploits reached England, and he was declared a pirate, with a price on his head. When Kidd eventually reached the island of Hispaniola in the Caribbean, he learned, much to his surprise, that he was a wanted man. He decided that he would return home and clear his name. He made a stop in Boston in July 1699, and was promptly arrested.

Kidd was sent back to England in irons, where he languished in prison for two years before he finally went to trial. The press had already painted him as the most black-hearted villain that ever trod a deck. The trial was a sham. Kidd was found guilty and condemned. He was hanged on May 23, 1701, and his body was gibbeted.

But what happened to all that plunder? Captain Kidd was one of the few pirates known to have actually buried treasure. Shortly after his arrest, authorities found a cache he had buried on Gardiner's Island at the eastern tip of Long Island, New York. They dug up 1,111 ounces of gold, 2,353 ounces of silver, and more than a pound of precious stones. A few years later two former members of Kidd's crew bribed their way out of prison and went straight to a place on the coast of Pennsylvania where they recovered a cache of gold worth 2,300 English pounds sterling.

Rumours abounded that there were more hidden caches of treasure: but where had Kidd hidden it? No one can say for certain just where Captain Kidd went between the time he left the Indian Ocean on a ship weighed down with treasure, and the day he arrived in Boston. Fortune hunters have looked for Kidd's lost treasure in the Dominican Republic, the eastern states of the U.S., New Brunswick, Nova Scotia, Prince Edward Island, and of course, Newfoundland.

Bennett's Grove, on the south side of Quidi Vidi Lake in St. John's is reputed to be the site where Captain Kidd buried five kegs of gold. The loot is supposedly in an unnamed gully that is protected by pirate ghosts. These unsavoury spirits confront anyone who goes near the place, whether they are treasure hunters or not. There is even a story that early in the twentieth century, some American adventurers found some of the gold and smuggled it off the island.

Ferryland, which has connections with pirates dating back to the days of Peter Easton, is also said to be a Kidd treasure site. Many people have allegedly claimed to have seen a ghostly pirate ship on the water there. One story even tells about a twentieth-century Ferryland resident finding a gold ring studded with diamonds. Was the ring part of Captain Kidd's treasure? If so, do pirate ghosts still watch over the hoard?

Oft Told Tales: Around the Island

The Ghost Train of Buchans

Railways first began operating in Newfoundland in 1882, and continued until 1988, when the legendary *Newfie Bullet* made its final run. Railroading in Newfoundland was part of the great age of steam-driven locomotives which saw the development of a distinct railroad culture. The positive elements of that culture focused on the binding of nations and island communities with roads of steel, technological marvels of engineering, and the romance of the railroad. But there was also a dark side: construction mishaps, train wrecks, robberies, haunted trains, and ghost trains. Sir Arthur Conan Doyle wrote a short story, "The Lost Special," about a train that disappeared without a trace.

In the late 1920s, the American Smelting and Refining Company constructed a twenty-two-mile rail line in the Newfoundland interior. The company was mining lead, zinc, and copper from the Buchans River country, and needed efficient transportation to carry the ore to the junction at Millertown. Not long after the line was completed in 1928, the Buchans River Dam burst and floodwaters swept away the wooden railway bridge that spanned the river. In the years that followed, more accidents plagued the Buchans-Millertown line. Some of them cost railway workers their lives.

In those days it was generally accepted that railroad work was dangerous. Accidents and even fatalities were unfortunate facts of life — but not phantom trains!

People who had made the run from Millertown to Buchans began telling stories about a ghost train. Passengers and crewmen alike said that they looked ahead along the rail line, and saw the light of another train coming straight at them! The sight was terrifying, because it looked as though they were on a collision course with a locomotive travelling at full speed. But at the very moment of impact, the mystery train would vanish.

What was the explanation for the apparition? Could all of those people have imagined the same thing? Some observers noted that the phantom train seemed to make its appearances only after there had been a fatal railroad accident. Was the spectre somehow connected to the spirits of dead railroad men? Trains no longer run on the island of Newfoundland, so there have been no reports of the ghost train for many years. But who can say for certain that it doesn't still make a midnight run on some isolated stretch of the old, abandoned line?

Lost in the Woods

Children who are tormented by nasty stepmothers, and find shelter and love in rustic cottages in the woods, are basic to the plots of many centuries-old folk tales, such as the Brothers Grimm classic *Hansel and Gretel.* But could such a story actually be true? John Mallory of St. John's, who died in 1952, frequently told friends and strangers alike a tale that he swore was a factual childhood experience with the supernatural.

John Mallory was born in the Conception Bay community of Silver Beach around 1880. When he was just three years old his mother, Mary, died. Over a year later his father, Jake, married a woman named Sarah. Jake's new wife did not like anything that could be a reminder of the departed Mary. She had Jake completely renovate the house so that it no longer resembled the one Mary had lived in. Sarah particularly resented little John, because he was Mary's child. Whenever Jake was away fishing, she treated the boy unkindly. John didn't tell his father about it.

When John grew big enough to do chores around the house, Sarah put him to work. If he wasn't quick enough, his stepmother complained to his father. John loved his father very much, but found Sarah's unfair complaints hurtful.

One miserable November day, when it was pouring freezing rain and Jake wasn't at home, Sarah told twelve-year-old John to go to the woods and collect firewood. By the time Jake returned home, it was dark and John had not come back. When Sarah told him she had sent the boy to gather firewood, Jake immediately became alarmed. He called on the neighbours for help, and soon searchers were scouring the woods. The temperature dropped, the rain fell harder, and the people found no sign of young John.

The next day, at about noon, Jake found John in a heavily wooded area. Not only was the boy alive and well, but he was also warm and dry. He didn't look at all like a child who had just spent a night lost in the cold, rainy woods.

John told his father that he had gotten lost in the darkness and the rain, and wandered around, crying out for help. Then he saw a house with a light in the window. A woman came to the door and invited him inside. It was warm and cozy in the house, and the woman let him stay all night, so he didn't have to go out in the cold, dark, and rain. The woman was very kind to him, John said, and he felt safe and warm in her presence. He left the house at daybreak.

Jake knew there was no such house in the woods. He asked John to describe the house and the woman. The description John gave of the woman was that of his departed mother. The house he described was his own home, the way it had looked when he was just a small child, and his mother was alive.

The Black Stag

Stories of ghostly animals are common all over the world and date back thousands of years. They can be found in Greek and Norse mythologies, and in the traditional stories of North American First Nations. In European lore they most frequently appear as demonic cats, dogs, horses, and wolves. British folklore has a devil dog known as Black Shuck, which is as big as a calf, has eyes of fire, and whose appearance always foretells misfortune and death. Black Shuck was allegedly the inspiration for Sir Arthur Conan Dolyle's Sherlock Holmes novel *The Hound of the Baskervilles*. It was probably not a coincidence that Sir Winston Churchill, who was plagued by periods of deep depression, called his affliction "the Black Dog." Animal apparitions usually have a few things in common: they appear unexpectedly; they cannot be harmed by guns or other weapons; and they leave sorrow behind them. In this Newfoundland ghost story, the phantom animal is a stag.

In 1804, a family named Conway lived at a place called Distress (now St. Bride's). The eldest son, Thomas, was a strong man and a skilled hunter. One day he set out to visit his father, who lived a few miles away in Point Lance. He loaded up a cart with produce, and hitched up his pony. He took along his rifle and powder horn in case he saw any game along the way.

About halfway to Point Lance, Thomas spotted a big, black stag in front of him. He quickly grabbed his gun and fired. Thomas was a crack shot, but to his astonishment the bullet had no effect on the stag. He reloaded and fired again. The animal stood unmoved. In frustration, Thomas loaded his gun with a double charge, and blasted at the stag once more. He *couldn't* have missed! But to his amazement, the stag was unharmed.

Now Thomas became afraid that there was something unnatural about the black stag. He hopped on the cart and drove to Point Lance as fast as the pony could haul him. When he told his father and some friends about the incident, they only laughed. They said it was obviously a case of poor marksmanship. At dusk, Thomas headed for home.

He never got there. About two hours after sundown, Thomas's wife saw the pony dash into the yard. Alarmed, Mrs. Conway alerted the neighbours and soon a search was underway. Thomas was found dead on the road. The contents of his powder horn had been poured over his face, but there was no mark of violence on the body. It was never discovered who — or what — had killed him.

Not long afterward, Thomas's wife set out for Placentia to have her child christened. With her were her brother-in-law and a friend. After the baptism, the group began the return journey to Distress. Like Thomas, they didn't make it. Their bodies were found in the same place where Thomas had died. Tracks in the dirt indicated that they had run around in blind terror. But whatever had killed them did not leave a trace. The mystery has never been solved.

The Ghost of Clarke's Beach

Everyone knows that one of the cardinal rules of water safety is never to go swimming alone. Another is not to swim after dark. All too often people ignore these basic bits of common sense and suffer the consequences. One such tragic incident lies behind the haunting of a popular swimming hole.

The community of Clarke's Beach is located on Conception Bay at the mouth of the North River. An old railway bridge, no longer in use, was a favourite spot for young people to swim in the river. According to local legend, one night a young woman went there to meet her boyfriend for a midnight dip. The young man didn't show up, so the girl decided to go for a swim anyway, alone in the dark. She drowned.

For years afterward, teenagers reported seeing something strange and frightening at the bridge. As they approached, they would see a dark form on the bridge. When they drew nearer, it appeared to be a young woman wearing a bathing suit, drying herself with a towel. Then the apparition would turn and look right at them with blazing red eyes. This terrifying experience was always enough to send the youngsters running.

It was believed that the ghost was that of the drowned young woman, returning to the bridge periodically to meet her boyfriend for their midnight swim. Perhaps she returns there still. If so, anyone swimming in the water below the old railway bridge at Clarke's Beach after dark might not necessarily be alone.

The Ghost of Holyrood

The final resting place of one's mortal remains has always been of considerable importance to the most powerful leaders of nations. Egyptian pharaohs had great pyramids, or were laid to rest in the exclusive Valley of the Kings; the bones of British monarchs have places of honour in Westminster Abbey.

For so-called lesser mortals, the final resting place is equally important, if not quite as ostentatious. Many favour a shady spot on a hillside, overlooking a river, in the company of family. Some choose the same pleasant real estate, but wish to be as far as possible from relatives. Whatever a person's reasons for the choice of a gravesite, that choice should be respected. If it is not, the individual responsible for the breach is liable to endure an unpleasant experience similar that of a Roman Catholic priest in the Conception Bay community of Holyrood.

An old Irishman named James Curran who lived at Holyrood had specific instructions about his burial. He did not want to be buried in the cemetery on the north side of the community, because the graves there would get flooded. He wanted to be buried in the graveyard on the south side, and he said if his wishes were not met, he would haunt whoever was responsible.

When Curran died, the local clergy decided his remains would be buried on the north side. Curran's family protested that this was against his final wish and that his ghost would come back to haunt them. The parish priest, Father Carm Walsh said, "We will bury this old Irishman in the north side burial ground, and I will take him over myself, and let him come back and haunt me." So, contrary to his last wish, James Curran was laid to rest in the north-side cemetery.

Soon after, Father Walsh was walking home from visiting parishioners when a snow storm blew in. Father Walsh got lost in the storm, and didn't arrive back home until the early morning. When he opened the door, there was James Curran's ghost, waiting for him. It was the ghost, people said later, that had led Father Walsh astray during the storm.

The very next morning, Father Walsh arranged to have James Curran's body moved to the south side burial ground. He blessed the grave, and said a special mass for Curran's soul. Curran's spirit was finally at peace.

The Corpse Light of Harbour Grace

Strange lights were often thought to be harbingers of misfortune. Swamps and marshes, which tend to be creepy places to begin with, were frequently marked as haunted because of mysterious lights seen at night. Among the names given to these lights were *will-o'-the-wisp*, *dead candles*, *jack-o-lanterns*, *jenny-burnt-tails*, and *ignis fatuus* (foolish fire — because only a fool would follow such a light). This was before people understood the properties of swamp gas, which can be luminous at night. What makes the following spook-in-a marsh tale unusual, is that a locally feared ghost actually acts as a benefactor, and the story takes place in the winter.

Not far from Harbour Grace was a place called Old Man's Marsh. People generally avoided the marsh because of a strange light they called the Corpse Light. It was believed that if you saw the Corpse Light, some misfortune, perhaps even death, would soon follow.

One winter day sometime around the turn of the twentieth century, the Reverend Canon Noel and his wife, residents of Harbour Grace, hitched their horse to their sleigh and drove to a blacksmith's forge several miles out of town. The smith fitted the horse with spiked horseshoes so it would be better able to manage the icy surfaces. He also sharpened the cutters to give the driver better control on the ice.

While the blacksmith was working on a runner, a bolt broke, causing an unexpected delay for Reverend and Mrs. Noel. By the time the repair had been made, it was dusk and snow was falling. The couple decided to make a dash for home.

By the time they drew near Old Man's Marsh, it was dark and the snowfall had become a blizzard. The horse struggled in knee-deep snow, and frequently went off the road. Finally, Reverend Noel had to get out of the sleigh and lead the horse himself. He lost all sense of direction in the driving snow, and soon they were lost. Noel and his wife shouted out for help, but their cries were lost on the howling wind.

Then Reverend Noel saw a light that he thought must be from a house. Leaving his wife behind him on the sleigh, he walked toward it for a better look. The light went out, and Noel could not see his way back to the sleigh. When he didn't return after a few minutes, Mrs. Noel became alarmed and began to ring the sleigh bells. Reverend Noel was able to follow the sound of the bells back to her.

They decided that they had better go back the way they had come. But they had trouble finding the road, and the horse tumbled over an embankment. The reverend had to unhitch the horse from the sleigh. He and his wife had to put the sleigh upright, before he could re-hitch the horse. Meanwhile, the icy wind was starting to bite through their clothing. If they didn't find shelter soon, they would freeze to death.

The chances of Reverend and Mrs. Noel getting out of their predicament alive were not looking very good, when suddenly they saw a bright light coming toward them. They thought somebody must have heard their cries and come looking for them. They shouted out again. The light came nearer, and then passed them by. They did not see or hear anybody.

Nonetheless, the Reverend reasoned that the light had to have been carried by someone who knew where he was going, so he and his wife followed it, with Noel once again leading the horse. Soon they came to a stone fence. They followed the fence to a house, and were overjoyed to see lights in the windows.

The family who lived in the house took the half-frozen couple in, and put their weary horse in the barn. They were given hot tea and food, warm, dry clothes, and a place to spend the night to wait out the storm. In the morning, the storm had blown itself out, and they could go home.

It was only as Reverend Noel and his wife were about to leave that they told their hosts about the strange light that had led them to the house. The people were not surprised about the light. It was well-known in that area as the Corpse Light. But it was considered by all to be an omen of bad fortune, not a guiding light for endangered travellers. They said, in fact, that local people wouldn't dare go outside if anyone had seen the Corpse Light. The one thing the Reverend Noel knew, however, was that whatever that ghostly light was, it had quite likely saved their lives.

Unless He Went Down Dead

This story has all the elements of a Gothic horror film. It includes a pair of brutal murders, a strange apparition on the road at night, and a hand reaching up from the grave. This melodramatic series of events began with an illicit affair and ended on the gallows.

In November 1870, the Geehan farmhouse on the outskirts of Harbour Grace was not a happy home. Patrick Geehan and his wife did not get along, nor was Geehan on friendly terms with his wife's brother, Garret Sears, who lived with them. Sears was a big man with a bad temper, and he was known to get rough with Geehan in family squabbles. In addition to this dysfunctional mix, Geehan was sexually involved with their domestic servant, Johanna Hamilton.

One day Mrs. Geehan found a bottle of rum that Patrick had stashed in the cellar. Enraged, she ran out to where he was working to confront him. The two got into a fight and in the heat of the dispute, Geehan wrapped his hands around his wife's throat and strangled her.

Geehan was terrified over what he had done. At that moment, his greatest fear was not being caught by the law, but by Garret Sears, who would soon return from his work in the field. Geehan convinced Johanna to help him prepare an ambush. While he sat in a corner of the kitchen with a loaded rifle, she was to watch for Sears returning from the field and signal when he was about to enter the house.

Sears came home from his work in the field, unaware that his sister was dead. As he approached the door, Johanna gave Geehan the signal.

The moment Sears opened the door, Geehan opened fire. He later told the police, "As soon as the shot was fired, he bawled and called me by name, then wheeled and fell down and, with the fall, stunned himself. I thought he was dead. I made sure he was dead. I wanted to put him out of his misery. I gave him one blow with the pole end of the hatchet and that's all. I didn't want to mangle or cut him up."

The next night they buried Mrs. Geehan in a shallow grave near a road about two miles from the farm. They hid Sears' body in a grave on the farm property, covering the spot with a pile of clay and manure.

Geehan told neighbours that his wife and brother-in-law had gone to St. John's to see a doctor. When his wife's body was found two days later, he feigned shock and grief. The seemingly bereaved Geehan said that he didn't know what had happened to his wife: she must have just dropped dead on the road. Sudden death wasn't entirely odd in the nineteenth century, and many of its causes were shrouded in mystery. But Geehan also had no explanation for the sudden disappearance of his brother-in-law. He probably hoped that everyone would think that the hot-tempered Sears had killed his sister and then absconded.

People were suspicious, though. At Mrs. Geehan's wake, some of them noticed bruises on her face and neck. Geehan also had scratches on his face, which he claimed were from cutting hay. But one woman recalled Johanna telling her that Mrs. Geehan would be dead by Christmas.

The local constable, Tobias Hackett, went to the Geehan farm a few days after the funeral. As Geehan looked on anxiously, Constable Hackett began to look around. He found a cart with bloodstains on it, as well as bullet holes in the tailboard. Neighbours told him that they had heard shooting from the Geehan farm the day Sears and his sister disappeared. That was enough for Hackett to arrest Geehan and Johanna and bring in men for a thorough search of the property.

In the days following the murders, wind, rain and scrounging animals had moved some of the manure and clay that had been thrown over Garret Sears' body. His hand was sticking up from the muck, as though beckoning to the police. They soon uncovered the body, and found bullet wounds in the chest and one arm; some fingers and an ear had been gnawed away by animals.

Geehan and Johanna were charged with two counts of murder. Geehan said that he had accidentally shot Sears while attempting to shoot a hawk. Sears hadn't died right away, he claimed, but Johanna had told him that to avoid trouble with the law, he'd better finish him off and handed him a pitchfork. "I did it," Geehan admitted, "and killed him." Of course, Johanna denied everything.

The two accused went to trial in St. John's on May 29, 1872. Among the witnesses was a man named Patrick Morrisey. His testimony included an account of a strange experience he'd had just after Mrs. Geehan's funeral, but before Sears' body was found.

He was on the road after dark with his wife and children. "I saw this man coming down the road, his face was pale, he looked queer. I got frightened. I said to myself, let Garret Sears be dead or alive, that is him … without knowing that anything had happened to him."

Morrisey said that he wanted to follow the man, who was heading toward Geehan's farm. But his wife and children were afraid and convinced him not to go.

The next day, Morrisey said, he met Geehan and told him about the incident. He asked Geehan if Sears had returned home. Morrisey said that Geehan had looked down and replied, "Sears didn't go down the road last night unless he went down dead."

Geehan asked if he thought Sears could have murdered his own sister. Morrisey replied that he had never heard of such a thing, but that he had heard of husbands killing wives and wives killing husbands. Morrisey then testified that in parting company, Geehan had cryptically said, "Farewell, now forever more."

He did not know why he said that.

Patrick Geehan was found guilty of the murders and was hanged. Johanna Hamilton served eight years in prison before being deported. As far as the law was concerned, the Geehan murder case was solved and closed.

But who, or what, had Patrick Morrisey and his family seen on the road that night? If his testimony was true, by telling Geehan about the apparition, Morrisey had startled the murderer into practically confessing his guilt when he said that Sears could not have been on the road "unless he went down dead."

The Town that Disappeared

This story comes from a member of a Newfoundland Paranormal Investigation Group who preferred to remain anonymous.

This tale began in a tiny village named Chance Cove, now a provincial park, which lies on Newfoundland's southern shore of the Avalon Peninsula. Chance Cove was once a potentially prosperous little settlement. Due to its location, they had little communication with the outside world, so they often had to rely on a carrier from a larger community to fill their orders and bring them supplies. The carrier that brought them their goods every few days would return again the day after for delivery, and had done so for many years. This was the same man that rode the beaten, wooded path by horse and buggy.

One day, after arriving in the town, the carrier merrily greeted the townsfolk and spoke with some of its citizens while waiting for the order to be filled. Once the man filled the order, he normally went on his way, not knowing what was about to meet his eyes when he returned. Upon his arrival the next day the carrier was surprised as he entered the town. The people he greeted everyday were not there. Thinking it odd, he immediately dismissed the thought, figuring they were inside their homes or near the water's edge. He continued on his way to his regular stop to drop off the supplies. But as he dismounted from the buggy to unload the cargo, no one came out to meet him and help with the offload. Puzzled, the man went to one of the homes to see if anyone was there. He knocked on the door a few times and no one answered. He looked in the window and saw no one around. He even called out, but to no avail. Now even more puzzled, the carrier checked all the other homes in the same manner, even opening doors and stepping in to check for any sign of inhabitants, but no one was around. Now worried, the man turned around, after checking the last house, to look out towards the town, and noticed that there were clothes left on the lines, buckets of water and wash water tipped over, and other items and tools scattered about. Even mounds of dirt that seemed to have been pounded away by someone or something gave the impression of a heavy struggle.

Now scared by the quick evacuation of the town, the man came to his own conclusion, and many more. He made haste back to his horse and buggy and sped away back to his town to notify the authorities. Investigations followed the man's claims but no detailed conclusions could explain what happened or why or how a whole town could disappear overnight. But from that day, late at night, if you stay in the park on or close to the site of the town, you can hear the screaming, wailing, and moaning of the settlers who once were there.

Disaster at Dead Man's Gulch

The following article, written by John W. White, appeared in the March, 1902, issue of the *Newfoundland Quarterly*.

Photograph by David Liverman; used by permission of the Geological Survey of Newfoundland and Labrador, Department of Natural Resources, Government of Newfoundland and Labrador.

Dead Man's Gulch, near Ferryland. Once a cave, it collapsed in 1823, killing forty-two fishermen seeking shelter from a storm. For many years after the disaster, the souls of the dead fishermen could be heard wailing whenever a tragedy was about to occur.

On the southwest of the narrows of Ferryland there's a deep gulch in the side of the cliff. The casual observer can see nothing extraordinary in this, and therefore does not make any enquiries. Nevertheless there's a sad story connected with it.

It's called by every fisherman "Dead Man's Gulch", and its history may be told in a few words. As it now appears it shows as if a semi-circular piece were cut out of the cliff extending from its top, inclusive, to its bottom to about two or three feet from the surface of the sea at high tide. In 1823 or thereabouts it did not thus appear. It was then a mammoth cave, with an entrance to the ocean, in and out from which fishermen were accustomed to go from time to time to secure bait fish that used to frequent the gulch.

But in the year of which I write, forty-two fishermen in about 14–15 boats entered the cave to avoid being swamped by a severe storm of wind and rain, accompanied by the usual heavy sea which had overtaken them while on the fishing ground. They ran as far as the cave, and there all took shelter. They waited for hours, but still the storm abated not.

As it grew late, peals of heavy thunder could distinctly be heard, but no one ever knew how these poor creatures listened and heard with fear and trembling. No one from shore could attempt a rescue; and even if they could, it is doubtful if they would, as no safer place than the cave could be thought of, as long as their food held out. But in the night, the watchers on shore heard a louder peal of thunder than the previous ones, and nearer, and then all was quiet. The distant rumbling previously heard still periodically went on, but there was nothing heard similar to the very loud and near one which had frightened them all so much.

When daylight came the wind had died away, and several set out to see how their friends in the cave had fared during the night. They arrived at the Gulch (as gulch it was then) and discovered that during the night its roof had fallen in, burying the 42 fishermen — not one having been rescued. None of the bodies were ever picked up, having been buried, no doubt, beneath the crushing mass of stone which had fallen on them. This had been the loud peal of thunder heard by the people during the night. The present floor or landing place of the Gulch, itself, is tenanted by saltwater pigeons, hundreds of them having nests in the cliffs on the side of the Gulch.

Because John W. White provided no sources for this story, no one has been able to corroborate it. If the disaster he described in such detail in 1902 was documented in 1823, the record has been lost. However, modern geological studies have shown evidence of a major cave collapse and rockfall at the site now known as Dead Man's Gulch. If the story White passed on to his readers is true — that in 1823, forty-two fishermen were killed when a sea cave in which they had sought shelter from a storm collapsed on them — then it ranks as one of the worst natural disasters in Newfoundland history in terms of loss of life. Its death toll was fourteen more than that of the tsunami that struck the Burin Peninsula in 1929. It also ranks as the third most deadly rockfall in Canadian history, after the Frank Slide of 1903 and the Quebec City Rock Slide of 1889.

For the people who live in the vicinity of Ferryland, there is no doubt whatsoever that the tragic story is true. What's more, according to local lore, for many years after the cave-in, the souls of the dead fishermen would warn of tragedies that were about to happen in Ferryland. For several nights in a row people would hear a strange howling coming from the Gulch. They said it sounded like the wailing of the wind mixed with human sobbing, and was enough to frighten the bravest man. That unearthly sound always heralded a death or some other misfortune in the community. It has been many years since that banshee-like cry has been heard in Ferryland, so perhaps the souls of those fishermen whose bones lie beneath the rocks of Dead Man's Gulch are at last at peace.

Case Files: Around the Island

Bad Dreams in the Basement

We often use the expression "haunted by bad dreams" when people endure a series of disturbing dreams that are connected to problems in their waking lives. But do bad dreams that seem to have no connection with an individual's real life qualify as "haunts"? And what if they come only when the dreamer is sleeping in a specific place, like a basement? Is it possible for a location's troubled past to somehow become an innocent person's nightmares? This story was sent to me in March 2010, by Marie, a Newfoundland-born woman residing in Mississauga, Ontario.

When I was born my family lived in a little house in the country. While I was still pretty young we moved to another place, but still in the sticks, so to speak. It was an old house, but me and my sister liked it because we had our own rooms. In the old place we had to share a room. Part of the basement was fixed up into a nice downstairs room. That was where I had the bad dreams.

Whenever we had family staying for a visit, I would lose my room. The company was always grandparents, or aunts and uncles, come for a weekend or Christmas or some holiday, and my room would be the guest bedroom. I slept on the couch in the basement.

I didn't mind that. I couldn't imagine Gran and Gramp trying to sleep on that couch when there was my nice bed upstairs. But I really did mind the nightmares.

Those dreams were horrible; truly horrible. Never in my life did I have such frightful dreams. I never had dreams like that when I slept in my own room. Only when I slept in the basement. I didn't dream about monsters or ghosts. I dreamed about myself doing real violent things, the kind of things that I would never do in a hundred years. One dream that I kept having was me beating the face off of my sister. I mean, I'd be beating her bloody, like I hated her. I dreamed about being chased by dead people and my legs wouldn't move to run. Sometimes I dreamed the police were taking me to jail, and I didn't know what for.

I would wake up with my pajamas soaked in sweat and my heart going a hundred miles an hour, and sometimes I wouldn't know where I was. But then I see that I'm on the couch in the basement room where we watch TV. If you looked in that room you would not think there was anything queer about it. It had a TV, a couch, and a couple of chairs. The walls were panelled, and there were tiles on the floor. But whenever I had to sleep down there, I had those awful dreams. The door at the landing was another thing.

To go up from the basement, there was a stairway that went up to a landing, and then you turned to another short stairway that took you to a hallway on the ground floor. The back door of the house was at that landing. It had a window in it. Sometimes in the night I would have to go to the bathroom, and the bathroom was upstairs. I was absolutely terrified to go past that door, even if I turned the light on. I had this dreadful feeling that someone was on the other side trying to get in. I thought that if I looked at the window I would see a face looking at me. Even now I get the willies thinking about it. If I had to pee really bad I would run up the stairs and past that window without looking at it. And when I went back downstairs I would look at my feet so I wouldn't look at the window.

I never told nobody about how scared I was to sleep in the basement, because I didn't want anyone to feel bad about putting me out of my room. One time I asked if I could have one of my girlfriends for a sleepover so

I wouldn't be alone down there, but Mum said we already had company.

This went on over quite a long time and it never failed. Sleep in the basement — bad dreams! Then one time my cousin Gordon came to visit. He never stayed the night at our house before, but that night he did. He was about twenty-one or two, and I was thirteen. Gordon said I didn't have to give up my room for him, that he'd be fine sleeping on the couch in the basement. He even made a joke that he didn't think he'd sleep very well in my room surrounded by all my girl stuff.

The next morning when he came up for breakfast, Gordon looked like he hardly had a wink of sleep. He told my dad, "Jesus, Unc, but I had the worst nightmare of me life last night, and I don't know what brought it on." Then he said, "This house ain't haunted, is it?" My dad looked surprised and said why would you ask that. Gordon said that in the middle of the night he needed to use the bathroom and that when he was going up the stairs he suddenly had this creepy feeling that someone was watching him through the window in the door. He said it made the hair on the back of his neck stand up.

Dad said, "I been up and down them stairs thousands of times and never felt nothing wrong." Well, after what Gordon said, I just had to speak up. I said to Dad that nobody but me was ever in that basement late at night, and I knew exactly what Gordon was talking about. Then I asked Gordon what his dream was. He said there was all sorts of crazy things, but what he recalled most was punching his girlfriend in the face over and over. Now Gordon wasn't the sort that would hit a girl, so a dream like that would really bother him.

I thought, well here's someone who knows what I've been going through and can back me up. So I started telling them about all the bad dreams I had down there, and how scared I was of the landing at the back door. Dad said everybody has bad dreams sometimes and when you wake up you should just forget about them because nobody ever got killed by a dream. Mum said I should just say an extra prayer to my guardian angel before I go to sleep. I didn't want to sound saucy, so I didn't tell her that I already tried praying to my guardian angel and Jesus, Mary, and Joseph, and anyone else I could think of, and it didn't do no good. The terrible dreams still came.

Sometime after that a neighbour was over. She'd lived around there all her life and knew everybody. Mum and her were having a cup of tea, and Mum told her what I'd said about the basement and the dreams and the landing, and also what Gordon had said. I didn't hear about this until much later, because my mother thought it might scare me.

The neighbour told my Mum that it all reminded her of a family that used to live in our house. The father was a bad one when he got into the liquor. He'd get into fights and even wound up in jail a few times. He'd belt the wife and kids around when he was drinking, and they were all scared of him.

Many a night he'd come home drunk, and he would always go in the back door. Sometimes he would wake up the whole house and the next day you could see that he hit the mother or the kids. Other times he just went downstairs to sleep off the booze. One morning the mother went down there after he was out half the night drinking. She found him on his cot, dead. He had lain down to pass out and died of a heart attack.

I am sure that basement room was haunted, and that was why I had those awful dreams. I think the reason me and Gordon felt scared on the landing was because that man's ghost, or something, was at the back door trying to get in.

Of course, that was a long time ago. My mother and father both passed on and me and my sister both moved away. I think that old house got torn down. But I know I will never forget the terrible nights I had in that basement.

Knitting Needles and a Corduroy Jacket

These beautifully told stories were sent to me by J.Y. Ferguson of Queen's Cove in March 2010. In an introductory note she wrote, "These two incidents happened to me, and I just relay the facts, and anyone is free to call it what they wish … but I swear to you that every word is true."

Photo by Wayne Butt, www.waynebutt.ca

The community of Queen's Cove, scene of the hauntings described by resident J.Y. Ferguson.

The Click of Knitting Needles

My parents and my husband and I shared this two storey, two apartment house, in a tiny community in Trinity Bay. The story I tell now is a private one, but I feel it's one worth passing on. It took place approximately eighteen months after my mother passed away, after a four year fight with cancer. Although the family had grieved and missed her, we also realized that she was so tired of her long struggle. It had ended and that she had finally found her peace.

She was a master knitter, and no pattern was too complicated for her to take on. Nearly every waking hour of those last years were spent sitting in her living room chair, with the click of knitting needles sounding like the second hand of a clock.

The laundry/furnace room is located in the lower apartment and one night, while alone in the house, I gathered a basket of laundry and was taking it to the washer. As I stepped through the kitchen door with my bundle of clothes, I heard the unmistakable sound of clicking knitting needles. The hall light was on, so as I looked up. It took a couple of seconds for my eyes to adjust. There she was, sitting in her favourite chair, with a partially made sweater hanging from her furiously moving needles. As I stared, she slowly raised her face and smiled, then returned to her task.

Some unknown noise, a creek of the house settling or the rattle of an air bubble in the heating pipes, broke my stare and I looked towards the sound. It was but for a second or two — when I looked back, she was gone.

As I write this, the image of her is still fresh in my mind, and I suppose it always will be. Her image was sharp and clear — not surrounded by a mist, nor did it wane, nor could I see through her, as (people) sometimes describe an apparition — she was just *there*!

I was not particularly thinking of her that evening. It was not the anniversary of her death, it was just an ordinary day and I was doing ordinary chores. That was over twenty years ago; I have not seen her since. I'm not prone to believe in ghosts or the paranormal, but there are things, in this world, that cannot be easily explained away — at least not yet. Perhaps she just wanted to let me know that she was free of the pain and the misery of cancer and in a better place.

The Man in the Corduroy Jacket

We live in a tiny community in Trinity Bay; a place where there is but one main road, everyone knows everyone else and are, more than likely, related, either by blood or marriage. Our house is located on a hill, not visible to the rest of the community. A long driveway leads from the house, around a blind turn, then down a fairly steep grade to connect with the main road and where our mailboxes are located. Directly across from those mailboxes is a two storey house, built around 1923 or 1924, and owned by my great uncle Harvey and great aunt Gertie. About forty or so feet from the house, was my uncle's work shed and it was a daily sight to see him, dressed in an old golden brown corduroy jacket and wearing a knitted toque, puttering about, doing his daily chores, going in and out of that shed with some tool or other in his hand.

Uncle Harvey was a gentle bear of a man whom everyone had great affection for. To our great sadness, that dear man developed dementia in his later years and, for some unknown reason, was always trying to find his way home, even though he had built the house himself and had lived in it ever since.

I well remember him coming to our house so many times, wanting one of us to drive him home, and wanting to know who was this woman who was always "following" him around. It was heartbreaking to see this dear, gentle old man so bewildered and lost and the stress he was causing his wife, who most of the time was in tears of frustration.

So one of us would take him for a drive a few miles along the highway, then pull to the side and ask him if he knew which way to go. He would always direct us back to his house, without one wrong turn and would be overjoyed when, rounding the last turn, his house would come into view.

For some unexplainable reason, when he entered the home, his brain would not process the familiar surroundings they had lived in for so many years, and refused to believe he was, indeed, home. Then the cycle would begin again. Sadly, or thankfully some would say, for him, he passed away.

Almost a year afterwards, I was walking down our driveway to retrieve the mail. Halfway down the hill, to my utter astonishment, I saw Uncle Harvey, dressed in his corduroy jacket and the toque on his head, step off the stoop of his back door and walk to his work shed and disappear inside.

Ghosts, goblins, and things that go bump in the night are not in my belief system, but with every fibre of my being, I *knew* I saw him! The only one I told was my mother; I had to tell someone! And I knew she wouldn't repeat it. However I was in for another shock just a week or two after this happened.

I was attending a baby shower and everyone was chatting, playing cards, oohing and aahing at how cute the baby gifts were; the usual itinerary for that sort of get together. Then I overheard a friend, who was playing cards the next table, telling the story of how several days before, she was taking her in-law's mail to them. They just happened to live in the house next door to the one in question, when she glanced to her left and saw Uncle Harvey walking from his back step to the shed. She said she knew it was him because he was wearing the corduroy jacket and toque. As crazy as it sounds, she said, I truly did see him.

I'm sure I didn't breath for minutes. I asked her about what day it was. The fact that we both saw an RCMP patrol car race through the community, with sirens roaring and lights flashing, a few minutes before Uncle took his walk, confirmed it was the same day, same time, same sighting.

We looked at each other, with one of those expressions that shows shock, disbelief and then, relief to know that we weren't both imagining things, but saw that dear old man, in his corduroy jacket and knitted toque. Perhaps he finally found his way home.

Dark Shadows

A few weeks after receiving the Knitting Needles and Corduroy Jacket stories from J.Y. Ferguson, I received the following from her by email.

This story was told to me by a ninety-three-year-old lady that I've known for about forty years. I know the house she's talking about. She doesn't mind me telling you the story, but she does not want her name or that of her sister used.

Many years ago, when she was first married, a woman and her new husband moved to a small rural community to build a home and raise a family. While waiting for the house to be built, they stayed in an old dwelling which was sometimes used as a summer cottage. It had no running water or electricity. Her younger sister came along to help out, and she brought her aging sheltie named Lady. Her husband's work took him away from home for days at a time, and she was glad for the company.

Water had to be brought from a well, heated on a wood burning stove, and the only source of lighting were kerosene lamps. It was a small house with a kitchen and sitting room on the ground floor, and two tiny bedrooms upstairs, separated by a landing of only four or five feet square.

Each night they would take the lamps up the narrow stairs — the woman in one bedroom, the sister and her dog in the other. A daily routine soon established itself. Work was proceeding on the new house, and there was hope of moving into it, with all the modern conveniences they were now having to do without, before the cool winds of autumn arrived.

However, one evening a frightening event would change their peaceful nights from then on. It was the end of another day, both took their lamps and went to bed, with Lady following behind. There was a crescent moon that night, casting some light into the house, but not much. Sometime during the wee hours of the morning, the sister was startled out of a sound sleep. The dog, who was friendly, passive, and never showed aggression, was pressed against the far wall, its teeth showing white in the dim light, and snarling. The girl was somewhat shocked. She had never seen Lady act like this. What the heck was wrong? She was staring at the doorway and would pay no attention to the command to be quiet.

Her owner followed the dog's line of sight, and there, standing in the doorway to the landing, was a dark figure. At first she thought it was her sister, and was a little annoyed at her for frightening not only the dog, but her as well. Then she thought something must be wrong, so she asked, "Are you alright? Did you have a bad dream?"

The figure did not answer, nor did it move, and Lady continued to snarl at it in obvious fear. That same fear crept through the girl's body, and she was about to cry out, when moments later the shadowy figure seemed to dissolve into the darkness. It didn't turn or walk away; it just seemed to fade away.

By this time the older sister had awakened and wondered what all the commotion was about. She lit her lamp and rushed across the landing to the bedroom. Her sister could not believe that she hadn't seen the figure. She would have had to pass right through it to get into the room! She tried to explain what she saw, and her sister would have put it to just being a bad nightmare, but for Lady's reaction. The dog had since calmed down and was curled on her blanket and back to her old gentle self. Everything was as it should be, except to say there was little sleep to be gotten for the rest of the night.

They never did find out what the apparition was. Nor did it return. But from that night, until moving into the new house, the lamps were left lit throughout the nights.

Gran's Sewing Machine

On March 25, 2010, about three weeks after she initially contacted me with two personal anecdotes about ghostly experiences, J.Y. Ferguson of Queen's Cove sent me this rather poetic account of a "ghost" known to the whole community.

In a small community, clinging to the cliffs on the coast of Trinity Bay, there is an old deserted house. In one of the windows at the front of the house that faces the sea, is an old foot-operated Singer sewing machine. There was one of these machines in almost every home, in years gone by. Much of the household linens and everyday clothes were made and repaired on one of those old Singers. They were very well made, reliable, and lasted a long time. In fact, I have one of my own, given to me by a friend, that was manufactured in 1926 and still works perfectly.

I've always loved these old Singers, and I suppose that's why I took notice of this one. The house had been deserted for many years, and I could not help but wonder why someone, a relative or neighbour perhaps, had not taken it, cleaned and restored it, as I did with mine.

The story, I was to learn, was that a fisherman, his wife, two sons, and his grandmother lived there. The sons grew into manhood and joined their father on his fishing trawler. Sadly, the wife passed away, but Gran was there to care for them and the household. They didn't have much, and Gran was always seen busy at her sewing machine, repairing their clothes, and making quilts for the beds out of material salvaged from otherwise worn out clothes.

Gran could be found almost everyday at the window, sewing and looking out over the Bay, waiting for the familiar shape of the trawler to safely return her "boys" home again. Fishing is a treacherous way of life, and there came a time when the father and sons left to haul their nets and never returned home. A sudden storm came from the northeast. It was a losing battle with the North Atlantic.

Fellow fishermen found the partially capsized trawler, but the three men's bodies were never recovered. The grandmother grieved terribly, and refused to accept that her family was lost. She could be seen, as always, in the window at her Singer, and looking out over the Bay. The dear old lady died a short two years later, never fully recovering from the loss of her "boys".

Many in the community, and others, say they've often passed by the house, and there she is, still sitting at her sewing machine, mending their clothes, and looking out over the Bay for her "boys" to come home. No one would ever take away her old Singer machine.

I Thought the Door Got Hit with a Sledgehammer

The following story was generously provided by eighty-two-year-old Bernard Maloney in Sweet Bay. The series of strange events that took place in the home in which he and his wife had resided for over forty years coincided with a period in which the wife was somewhat invalided. Poltergeist activity has usually been associated with the presence of an adolescent — most frequently female — in the "haunted" house. However, there have also been instances of poltergeist-like disturbances in places that have been the scene of great emotional stress, brought on by such intense personal trials as illness and bereavement. In this story, the narrator tells of apparitions, mysteriously misplaced objects, and a presence that violently objected to being told to "stay put."

About seven years ago, one morning after I finished breakfast, and when I was coming in the living room about 5:30, my wife was standing in the living room, and I knew she was still in bed. And she faded away. When I got in the living room she was standing by the bedroom door looking out at me, and again she faded away. She had crippled legs, and not having been in the basement for about seven years. One morning after seeing her I went down to light the fire, and I had two brooms, one in each end of the basement. On this morning, they were in one end put together. I asked her what she was doing in the basement. She said, "I never been in the basement."

The next morning when I went down, a can of diet Coke was on a paint can, opened up. I went and looked and about one inch was gone out of the can. The next morning there was about one inch left in the can. The next morning I went down, a fishing line that was hanging in one end of the basement was on the floor in the other end. Tools I had down there would be moved.

In the morning when I would be getting the fire lit I would hear someone walking in the hall. I would come up and the wife was still in bed. When I would go to bed at night, I would see shadows coming in the hall. One night, one came in about the height of a dog walking on all fours, but no head. The next night I closed the door in a spare room, and I said, "If you are in there, stay in there tonight," and I went in the bathroom to wash, and I thought the door got hit with a sledge hammer because it flew open.

One night while the wife was in hospital, at four in the morning, I went to the washroom and just as I got in bed someone started to move me over. And I am telling you, this is nerve breaking.

Also, I had a moose licence and went every morning, and the morning I seen the moose, I went to pull the hammer back, and no tension on the hammer. I came home, took the stock off, and the screw broke right off. I had a twelve gauge shotgun, and sometimes the empty shell would stick, and my cousin gave me his to use. I put it in the basement. One day he came to get it, and when he went to use it there was there was no tension on the hammer. I had to take the stock off to fix it. This same cousin came down to get the loan of a staple gun. He tried it in the basement, put it in a plastic bag and went home and used the staples that was in it, and went down in his basement to get more and when he came up to put them in, the spring was gone. He phoned and told me. I said don't worry, I got another one. About three weeks later I was up in my workshop cleaning up, and under a pile of junk the spring (of the staple gun) that he carried home was there. He lived about 500 yards from me.

What I am telling you is true. We are living in this house forty-six years. I built it myself, and only about seven years ago this started. My wife passed away in January 2010, and I haven't heard anything since.

I Just Come by to Say Goodbye

Can a person who is passing from this world to whatever lies beyond somehow make contact with a loved one many miles away? This story was sent to me by email in March 2010, by a retired resident of St. John's. He prefers to remain anonymous, for family reasons.

First I want to say that I always believed in God, and I always believed we have a soul that goes somewhere after death, somewhere good I hope. But I never used to believe in stuff like ghosts and forerunners and the supernatural. Nobody in our house did, because our father said it was all foolishness.

My brother Tom was eight years older than me. He went away to Toronto about 1955. I went there too for a year or so, but then I came back here, not liking Toronto very much. Me and Tom kept in close touch all the time. He used to come back to visit in the summer.

Tom got cancer, and in the last few months of his life he was pretty sick. One day in September 1990, we got a phone call from Toronto. It was Marg, Tom's wife. She said he took a real bad turn, and the doctor said he didn't have long to go. I said I'd be on the next plane to Toronto.

We called my son to get him to arrange a flight for me, because the wife and I didn't know much about that. He called back and said he had me booked on a flight to Toronto the next day, that was the best he could do, and he would pick me up in the morning and drive me to the airport. So Vy, my wife, packed me a suitcase so I'd be all ready to go.

That night I didn't sleep very good, just thinking about poor Tom. And I was feeling really bad because I thought maybe I wouldn't get there in time to see him one last time. In the morning I was sitting on the edge of my bed, and I was looking at the clock on the dresser, thinking about how much time I had before Jack (my son) would be here for me. Vy was out in the kitchen.

What I tell you now is the truth, so help me God. I was looking at the clock. It was just after quarter past six. When standing there right in front of me was my brother Tom. He was wearing blue pajamas, and it looked like he had just got out of bed, just like me. When we were boys he used to call me Little Brother, though he stopped it when we got older. But that's what he called me there in our bedroom, while I was waiting to go to the airport. He said, "Little Brother, I just come by to say goodbye." Then he was gone.

Now I know what you must be thinking; I was still half asleep and I dreamed it. But I wasn't. I had already been up and gone into the bathroom, so I was wide awake. And I didn't have anything to drink the night before. I saw him and I heard him, and I would swear on the Bible that was my brother Tom.

But that isn't all. Not ten minutes later the phone rang. It was my nephew, Tom's son, calling from Toronto to tell us that Tom died just a few minutes ago.

I believe Tom came to see me right when he died, because I wouldn't make it in time to see him. He was always the one to come here and see me, and he did it one last time. Of course I went to Toronto for the funeral, and they said it was a shame I didn't get to see him once more. I told them that I did, but they all said I must have dreamed it. That's what they all still think. But Tom and I know better.

Two Ghost Stories

The following stories came to me by post from Rex Sterling in Pasadena, Newfoundland. They were accompanied by a letter which makes an excellent introduction.

I have had a few experiences with ghosts and have written about them, (two examples enclosed). I've never been frightened by these experiences, but intrigued. I think those who have gone to "the other side" can communicate with the living through vivid dreams.

Those who are receptive or "tuned in" have the ability to see a ghost in spiritual form. My father who passed away in 1951 has appeared to me many times. These have been benevolent occasions which I welcome.

Sometime before my brother died, he promised if it were possible, he would "contact me" after his death. He died on February 13 this year, and I await his appearance in hopeful anticipation.

You may be wondering if ghosts speak? Yes they do, not verbally but mentally. That's how they communicate.

The Fishing Trip

My best friend Mike and I had been planning our fishing trip for weeks, and I was really disappointed when he had a slight accident on the job and couldn't go. He insisted I go alone. I was reluctant, but the weather was ideal for fishing so I packed up my gear, got in my SUV, and headed for our favourite pond. I was backing my vehicle down to the water's edge to launch my boat, when I heard a strange but somehow familiar sound.

I looked up to see an old car slowly coming down the dirt road leading to the pond. It was a vintage Ford Model-A. I hadn't seen one of those outside of an old car show, or on TV, in years. As it got closer, I could make out the licence plate; Newfoundland 1921. I stopped what I was doing to watch.

The car stopped some distance away and a young man who I guessed to be in his thirties got out. His clothes were way out of date. *It must be part of a promotion*, I thought. He's dressed like they did in the 1920s, the same vintage as the old Ford. He started taking his fishing equipment out of the back seat, then ambled down the sloping bank towards me.

"Good morning," he said cheerily. "Ideal day for fishing, isn't it?" I wondered where his boat was. Shoreline fishing was no good at this pond. Then a thought struck me, "I hope he doesn't ask me to take him out in my boat."

"Are you going out alone?" he asked.

"Oh no, here it comes," I thought. But why not? He will be company for me, and I'll find out about the old Ford and his clothes.

"You can join me if you like," I said. His face lit up at my invitation. "Ah yes," he sighed. "It will be nice to finally get home again." Home? What did he mean? I didn't question him. I launched the boat, and we rowed out to the middle of the pond. We sat there for the longest time in silence without a single bite. I was getting bored and discouraged. I was about to row back to shore when my strange companion said, "I want you to bring me over there." He pointed to the deepest part of the pond, about fifty yards away.

I did as he asked. Suddenly the fish began biting and soon my creel was full. "You sure brought me luck," I said.

"It's just my way of repaying you for bringing me back home," he said.

There he goes again. I was getting nervous. This guy is some kind of a nut. He looked at me intently as if he knew what I was thinking. *What the hell was he talking about? There are no cabins around here!*

"I was fishing in this very spot in 1921," he told me. My mind raced. 1921? That was over eighty years ago. This guy was maybe thirty-two, thirty-three. He was a nut for sure.

"I know you think I'm crazy, but I'm not," he said. "I was drinking. I fell overboard and drowned."

I began moving away from him. He pointed to the water. "I've been down there ever since. I keep coming back to my starting point on the far shore. Each year on the anniversary of my accident I come back to my starting point looking for someone to bring me home. Nobody has until now."

My god! This guy is as crazy as a bedbug. He's going to kill me for sure. I had to get this nut case out of my boat and I had to do it soon. Before I could do anything, he began to fade away right in front of my eyes. What was happening to me? I was shaking like a leaf in a wind. Somehow I managed to row back to shore. There was no sign of the old car or any tire tracks except the ones I had made. I couldn't wait to tell Mike as soon as I saw him.

"I've never known you to have an overactive imagination, old buddy," Mike said. "There's a way of finding out what you told me is true."

"There is? How?"

"We will go down to the library or newspaper office tomorrow and see if they have a record of a drowning accident back in 1921. If they do, we will find out if it was the same pond and the same person you had in your boat." We did go down to the library, and it was.

The Helpful Ghost

In the early 1980s, the company I worked for transferred me from St. John's to their branch office in Corner Brook. My wife remained behind until I found a suitable place for us to live. I was lucky to locate an ideal, fully furnished two-bedroom apartment on the west side. When the moving truck arrived from St. John's, I called my wife to say she could join me in a few days.

Our landlady was a pleasant woman, a widow in her late sixties, I guessed. She had lost her husband, Victor, to cancer some years before. The apartment I rented had been closed up since the death of her bachelor brother, Edward: the last tenant to live there. I should have asked what happened to him, but was too preoccupied with getting settled in and having my wife join me.

I paid the first and last month's rent, and after work began unpacking numerous cartons and boxes. It was tiring work, so I stepped outside for a smoke. I didn't notice the old man approach, but there he was. He said his name was Ned. He had once lived in the apartment. I should have made the connection then and there, but didn't.

As we talked, I told him how I hated unpacking. He offered to help, but I was reluctant to accept, as he looked much too frail for the job at hand. But I invited him in anyway. I was amazed at the effortless way he worked. For such an elderly man, he had unlimited stamina. There was one room in the apartment he flatly refused to enter: the master bedroom. I thought it odd, but I didn't ask why.

Two days later my wife arrived at Deer Lake Airport. On the drive to Corner Brook, I told her all about Ned, and how he had been so helpful in getting me settled in. I described him in detail. Of course, she was anxious to meet my benefactor and thank him personally, but I suddenly realized I hadn't asked Ned his last name or where he lived. But I was sure he'd come round for a visit when he learned my wife was here.

Our first night in our new apartment was a restless one. We both slept fitfully. The room was freezing, despite our having turned the thermostat to its highest setting. I made a mental note to speak to the landlady about it first thing in the morning. I was at work that morning when I received a frantic phone call from my wife begging me to come home as soon as possible.

When I arrived at our apartment, my wife was standing on the front steps trembling and pale faced. At her feet was a suitcase. "What's the matter, darling?" I asked. "You look like you've seen a ghost, and what's with the suitcase?"

She was hysterical and on the verge of tears. "We're leaving here right now. I'm not staying in this place another minute. I'll wait for you in the car."

After calming her down, I asked what had happened to get her so upset. She said she had been in our bedroom dressing, and saw the image of an old man in the mirror. She knew it was old Ned because of the description I'd given her. Thinking he had somehow managed to get into the apartment, she turned to confront him, only to have him vanish before her eyes. She began screaming.

The landlady, hearing her screams, came running to see what was the matter. My wife told her what she'd seen and the colour drained from our landlady's face. "She was very reluctant to tell me," my wife said, "but broke down and told me the old man I'd seen in the mirror was her late brother Edward. He took his own life in our apartment, died in the same bed we slept in last night. My God, it's all so horrible."

"But why would our landlady tell you all that?" I asked. "She never said a word to me when I rented the place. Besides, it's crazy. I swear the old gentleman who helped me unpack was as real as you and me. There's no way he could have been a ghost. Your imagination is working overtime, dear."

"You think so? Then I'll prove it to you."

We drove to a local cemetery, walked a short distance to an older section of it. "Look there," said my wife, pointing to a headstone which bore a fading picture of the old man who had helped me unpack. Looking closer I could easily read the birth and death dates. "I don't understand any of this," was all I could say.

"I know what I saw," said my wife, still visibly upset. "But why would our landlady keep such a dreadful thing from us?"

"I imagine she kept it a secret out of fear of never being able to rent the apartment again. It was closed up since his suicide." My wife shuddered. "We were out-of-towners and I guess she never thought we'd find out about it except for …"

"Except for what?"

"Her dead brother's visit to me in our bedroom this morning."

I returned to the apartment later that day to collect our belongings. The landlady was quite contrite and upset over the turn of events. It was easy to see why she was as shaken by it all as was my wife. She offered to return our deposit. I accepted.

Before leaving I gave her my solemn word that I would never mention the episode to anyone; her secret was safe with me. My wife and I now live in Pasadena. On those occasions I have to go to Corner Brook, I'll drive by our old apartment to see if anyone is living there. No one ever is.

Three Mystic Experiences

The following stories came to me in a letter dated March 2010, from Rita M. Alexander of Burin Bay Arm. While only one of the three experiences she describes is, strictly speaking, a ghost story, the other two are certainly extraordinary.

A Picture of Dad

My father, Herbert J. Eddy of Garden Cove, passed away suddenly on the evening of February 26, 1973. He was just under three months short of his fiftieth birthday, which would have been on May 6. At the time of my dad's passing, I was the young mother of two little girls, with the hope of having a son sometime in the future.

In the summer of 1979, I was vacationing with my family at my childhood home in Garden Cove. One evening, I was lying in bed reading, when suddenly there flashed before my eyes a picture of my dad. This picture was so clear and life-like, I could see the sparkle in his blue eyes, and he was smiling the most beautiful, open smile I had ever seen on his face. In his arms he held a beautiful baby boy. My son was born nine months later on the May 6, 1980! What a precious gift! My dad knew, loved, and held my son even before I did. I know beyond the shadow of a doubt, my father is my son's guardian angel!

A Paper Cross

My mom, Dorothy Frances Eddy passed away on June 3, 1989. On Mother's Day 1990, I was at work in the Labrador City Public Library in Labrador City. There were very few visitors to the library that day, so to keep myself busy, I decided to tidy the bookshelves. As I scanned the shelves and straightened some books, I randomly pulled a book from the shelf. Immediately as I did this, a piece of paper fell from the pages onto the floor. I bent down to retrieve the paper, and lo and behold, what I held in my hand was a paper cross inscribed with the following words:

> On Mother's Day
> "the Lord bless thee, and keep thee
> The Lord make His face shine upon thee,
> And be gracious unto thee"
> Num. 6: 24, 25

I turned the paper over to see if there might be something written on the back. There was not. Out of a collection of approximately thirty thousand books, why did I choose that one particular book, on that one particular day? Chance, some might say, but I would not agree. My heart was aching on that first Mother's Day without Mom. I believe this was sent to comfort me, and it surely did. I still have the little cross. It is my most precious keepsake.

One Single Red Rose

On May 20, 2004, I was suddenly awakened from my sleep at about 4:00 a.m. with chest pain. At the Dr. GB Cross Hospital in Clarenville, I was diagnosed with a heart attack. On March 4, 2005, I was preparing to leave home for the Health Sciences Centre Hospital in St. John's, where I would undergo heart bypass surgery the next day.

Prior to leaving I had prayed to my favourite saint, Saint Theresa (the Little Flower), that my surgery would be successful and I would make it through okay. It is believed that if you ask the Little Flower for a sign, she will send you a rose if your wish or desire is to be granted.

I was at the Ultramar Gas Station in Burin, filling my car with gas just prior to leaving for St. John's, and I still hadn't received a rose. I have put gas in my car hundreds of times over the years without spilling any, but that morning I spilled it over my hand and the sleeve of my coat. Upon entering the station to pay for my gas, I asked the attendant if there was somewhere I could wash my hands. Imagine my surprise and joy when I entered the washroom, and the very first thing my eyes beheld was one single red rose sitting in a white vase on the washbasin! A gas station washroom! Off I went on what I would say was the most light-hearted journey I had ever undertaken. You see, I had my answer just in time! Needless to say, everything went well, without any complications of any kind.

I suppose many of today's generation would say: "We see what we want to see." But I say, as the Bible says, "He that hath eyes to see, let him see; he that hath ears to hear, let him hear."

I Refused to Be Scared of My House

This story came to me by letter, and is quite chilling. At the author's request, I have changed the names of the people involved. I have also not given the name of the town, since it is a small community, and the author was concerned that the house might be branded as haunted, becoming a target for Halloween pranks.

The events in the story cover a most unusual time in our lives that affected the whole family, the task of rethinking it to put it on paper is a little unnerving and frightening again. It involves three members of my family: my sister Jane, my mother, and me. My father worked at sea, so he wasn't home all the time. But he did acknowledge that something was happening in the house and he could sense our fear.

To give you some background, we had a beloved beagle named Lady that died in August 1975. She was killed by a drunk driver, which made her death all the harder.

The haunting started in 1976, about a year after Lady's death. I am sure that what we heard in our house the first three times was the spirit of an animal, and that it was Lady. The fourth time I don't know what it was, and what was left behind to this day I'm not sure of either. We have come to live with some of it and ignore the rest. There have been several times over the years that we heard a few noises again, but best to ignore it and it will go away.

The first incident happened to me.

I was in the living room watching TV. Mom was out in the kitchen, out of earshot. When she was alive, Lady had been allowed to lie on the couch, and she always favoured the same end. I was following the show on TV when I just became aware of a different kind of noise in the room. I turned down the volume to listen, but didn't hear anything out of the ordinary. As I started to turn up the volume I again caught a noise coming from over by the couch. Out of curiosity I got up and went to see what could be making that noise, when suddenly there was a loud snort, just like a dog makes in his sleep, only louder. That stopped me in my tracks, because I immediately recognized the sound as one Lady used to make when she slept. The noise was exactly in her spot on the couch. I felt a chill come over me when I realized that there was a heavy breathing coming from the same area. This was unusual; I couldn't believe I was hearing something so strange. I went closer to the couch, staring at the end, and just listened. Sure enough, the breathing continued, rhythmic, like a sleeping dog. I didn't really feel afraid, as she had been a loveable animal, and wouldn't have hurt any of us. But this was very strange and unsettling.

I stared at the couch, intently listening, when suddenly the fabric on the couch moved as if something settled. Well, I tell you, I stepped back a few paces with that. I sensed that this was Lady, but the dog was dead and shouldn't be there. It went on for about fifteen minutes. I never told my mother, as I was afraid it would scare her. But I did tell my sister Jane a few days later, and it didn't phase her one way or the other.

A few weeks later I was in the living room watching TV again, but this time Jane was also in the room. We were alone in the house, and I had put the first experience aside (but not forgotten it), as I hadn't heard anything for three weeks, and supposed it was a one time occurrence.

Again, we were watching TV when I heard the noise. I guess I had been tuned to it, because I heard it just as it happened. This time it was just the breathing. At first I never said anything to Jane, but as I looked at her to see if she had noticed, her head turned towards the end of the couch, and she started to hear the breathing. This time it was much louder, and when she looked back at me, I whispered, "That's it. That's the noise I was telling you about."

Just as I said it, the breathing stopped. Jane got up and went over to the couch, putting her hand in the area. When she touched the couch, the breathing started again. It was a different noise this time, exactly like a dog snorting while turning over to get her belly rubbed, which is what Lady would have done. Jane jumped back into her chair, and the two of us listened in silence, listening to the breathing on the couch until it ended sometime later.

We decided a few days later to tell Mom. Mom believed in the spirit world, but it just seemed to be too out of this reality to be happening to us in our home. Again, we put it aside until about a week later, when the three of us were watching TV. All of these occurrences happened at the same time of night, around eight o'clock. This time Mom heard it first; she suddenly told us to listen. The breathing was happening again, and she was stunned at what she was hearing. It was a little chilling, to say the least. I think Mom did get frightened when she realized this was what we had told her about, and now she was experiencing it herself.

We all agreed that it did sound like Lady. I think that's what was so amazing about the whole thing, that Lady came back to us three times to have a snooze on the couch. We never felt afraid, since it was Lady. But we did feel that she shouldn't be there, and wondered how and why she was. The scary thing about it was that there was something in the house from somewhere unseen that shouldn't be there.

We didn't hear the breathing again for some years. At the time, I wasn't even sure that it was breathing. It could have been the house settling and sounded similar. A few times there was a definite snort and breath being let out. But it sure felt the same, and each time it happened it gave me a little jump with fright. Since we weren't hearing it, we began to believe that it was gone.

It was about a month later, and everything was normal again. We weren't "listening" all the time, or stealing glances at the couch every time we passed it. This one evening I was in my bedroom with a friend from another community. We had been friends for a few years, but I hadn't told her or anyone else about the haunting. We were sitting on my bed just talking. I was kind of leaning backwards against the pillow, strumming my guitar while we talked, when over by my door, down near the floor, I picked up on a breathing sound again. I stopped playing, and I think I held my breath, listening.

I must say, this one made me afraid. This was not Lady. This was something else. This felt bad, evil! It was a breathing, but it was fast and raspy; like a breathless pant. My friend heard it, too. I could see the fear in her eyes, and she asked me what the noise was. At first I said I didn't know, but I knew what it was immediately.

The panting started to move across the floor. You could follow the sound with your eyes. My friend was definitely afraid, and begged me to tell her if I was doing it. She jumped up closer to me on the bed, and we "watched" the noise continue to cross the floor, then jump up on the end of my bed and sit there, watching us.

Well, we were bloody frightened out of our minds, trembling with fear. We started to move to get off the bed, when next thing, the breathing jolted from the end of the bed, ran up the length of me, and stopped at my face. I could feel its breath on my face and a little weight on my chest, and my hair puffed backwards with each pant. I was terrified and couldn't move. *Something* was sitting on my chest and holding me there, two inches away from my eyes!

My friend grabbed my hand and yanked me off the bed. The two of us ran screaming out of my room and down the hall to the living room where Mom was. As I explained what happened, she looked at us and could see our fear, and knew something was back. We had to go back down to my room to see what the hell had happened. My friend was too afraid to come with us.

My door was now closed, and when we entered, we listened for a second, and sure enough the panting was still going on, this time sitting on my pillow. I remember being behind Mom and starting to shake uncontrollably. I felt like I was being watched, and afterwards Mom said the same thing.

We were afraid to approach the bed, as there was something there for sure. So we just left the room and closed the door again. This sound wasn't the same thing we had heard the three times in the living room.

That night I got into bed with Mom. We made Jane get in, too, as we were very scared that it would happen to her in her room. Dad was away on his shift, so we were very nervous in the house by ourselves.

We eventually told Dad what had happened, but each time he ventured into the room, nothing was going on. I tried to reason it out, that possibly, maybe the three of us could be imagining it. But I knew in my gut it was truly real. What convinced me was that my friend, who hadn't heard the story of the couch breathing, didn't know anything about what was going on. But she had heard something in my bedroom, and it frightened her. So, that couldn't have been my imagination.

For the next month and a half, we would check my room each day and the breathing was still there. It was mostly on the bed, but on other occasions it would be over by the window, sitting on the floor, or up on a shelf. One time, it met me at the door.

I slept on the couch, the same one where we first heard the breathing, for that whole time. Then suddenly, it was gone. My friend had returned for visits, but never did go to my bedroom ever again. I checked my room each day after that, and there was nothing. It felt like it left us, but I continued to sleep on the couch for another two weeks until I was brave enough to sleep in there again. I moved my room around, and I used a night light for the next five years that I continued to sleep there. I also slept with the door open for the first few months. Only once over the years did I hear the sound again in my room, over by the door. But I refused to be scared of my house, and I had no choice but to ignore it.

Even though the breathing had stopped, and I hoped that it was gone, there remained this unsettling feeling that there was, and still is, something in our home. It started a few months after the bedroom incident, with little things. One night, I was going to bed and I brought a slice of toast in with me. I had to leave the room for a minute, and put the toast on my night stand. When I came back, the toast was torn up in bits on my bed.

I had become used to unexplained things happening, so each time something did, it was a little less frightening. Your hair would suddenly blow back from your face. Not strongly; just enough to move your hair. That happens to this day. We would smell things like flowers or perfume. Things would be moved. A picture would be down on the floor. Not fallen down; just laid there, and when we hung it up, it would be down again; things like that.

A few summers ago, we had the front door open to let in some air, when this cat jumped in and ran down the hall. I yelled at my sister that a stray cat had gotten in, and we searched the house but couldn't find it. We both had seen it, and it had moved very fast. It was not one of our own cats, as they would have come when we called. Since then we have seen glimpses of the cat, and at times felt it touching our legs, and heard it coming down the stairs. It's still here, but we haven't seen anything for a while.

Other times our own animals would become afraid, and back away snarling and spitting at something they were sensing. Our second beagle frightened me so bad one night, barking and growling at something in the kitchen, that I phoned my cousin and asked him to come over and stay with me until the rest of the family came home.

One of our cats had kittens in the closet, and I was sitting on the floor playing with the newborn kittens when suddenly she arched her back and began hissing at something. She was looking over and up at the window. I ran out and told Mom about this. The cat moved her kittens within an hour to another room. But the one thing that really frightened me was when I was washing the dishes, and I heard someone walk very rapidly up behind me, very close to my back. I could feel something there behind me until I finished the dishes.

My next-door neighbour got a fright one day, and won't come into this house by herself ever since. It was daytime, and there wasn't anyone in the house. It's customary to leave your door unlocked when you're going on short errands, and she had come into the house thinking we were home. She called out to us, but there was no answer. So she went to the phone to call my sister for a chat until one of us came home. She told us afterwards that as she went into the living room for the phone, she heard something upstairs in my the home office. She heard loud footsteps, like a woman in high heels walking across the floor. So she went down the hall towards the stairs leading up into my office, thinking that I was up there and hadn't heard her come in. She started to climb the stairs, but stopped and called out my name. Footsteps walked across the floor towards my office door and then stopped. She called my name again, and when no one answered she bolted out of the house.

I have heard those footsteps several times myself, though never upstairs when I'm there, but when I'm in the living room or the kitchen. The funny thing is, the footsteps start in the attic and go into my office. Lots of times we hear thumps up there, and the plants grow funny. I have a six-foot geranium growing, and a head of romaine lettuce that grew three feet and sprouted yellow flowers.

My father and mother have both passed away in the years since the breathing, but Jane and I have moved back into the house. My mother used to wear bobby pins in her hair, and to this day we continue to find bobby pins in places where they hadn't been ten minutes before. We feel sometimes that she's here, but I think that's mostly wishful thinking.

That Was Mother

Blood may be thicker than water, but how well do family ties transcend the barrier between the living and the dead? This story comes from a resident of Sydney, Nova Scotia, who prefers to remain anonymous. The narrator of this tale knew little about her forebears, yet someone from a past generation wanted to see her.

I have lived in Nova Scotia all my life, but my mother and father both came from Newfoundland. I never met any of my grandparents and I never knew much about them. I know that my dad's father died when he was still a very young boy, and so Dad didn't get any education because he had to work. Mother used to have to do the bills that came in the mail because Dad couldn't read them. After Mother died, I did them.

I never knew anything about my grandmother, my dad's mother. We didn't even have a picture of her. We never talked much about those things. I just know that she died before I was born.

Then one night something happened to me that I will never forget.

I was in bed asleep. Suddenly I was awake, or I thought I was. I saw a woman standing by my bed. She looked old, and her dress was like something you see in old photographs from Victorian times. She was right by my bed and she was just looking at me with this real stern expression. She didn't say a thing, just looked.

She looked like a solid flesh and blood person, but I knew she wasn't. I got a real good look at her face and her old-fashioned clothes. I was scared, but I couldn't move. Then she just disappeared. I wanted to crawl under my bed, I was some scared. I didn't even have the nerve to get out of my bed and run to my father's room. I just pulled the blankets over my head.

I told my dad about it in the morning. He said I had a nightmare, but when I said the woman was really there, he thought for a moment and then asked me what she looked like. I told him, and he just went white. He said, "That was Mother."

I said it couldn't be. It didn't look at all like Mother, and if she could come back from the dead she would never, ever scare me like that. Dad said, "Not *your* mother; *mine!*"

For the rest of his life my dad believed that was his mother that came to my room that night. I never saw her again. I think she just wanted to see me once. And I think that hard look on her face was like a warning to me that I better behave myself.

The Flatrock Fires

Poltergeist activity is usually associated with loud noises, disappearing objects, moving furniture, and breaking dishes and other fragile items. It has also been connected to the frightening phenomenon of fires that break out unexpectedly for no known reason. The following is a Canadian Press news report published in the Niagara Falls *Evening Review*, December 11, 1954.

> The RCMP was asked to investigate the outbreak of mysterious fires in the home of Mike Parsons at Flatrock, north of Carbonear, on Conception Bay. Officers failed to determine the reason for the rash of flames and so informed the Attorney-General.
>
> Over a two-week period the five members of the family were alarmed when the following incidents occurred at intervals of two or three days. A dictionary burst into flames for no apparent reason. A sack of sugar ignited of its own accord. A box of religious literature, stowed in an upstairs bureau, turned into a bonfire. A blaze appeared under the eaves of the house. The floorboards in one room of the house flared up. Finally, a doll was consumed in flames.
>
> While the mysterious fires were small and easily extinguished, the family members were understandably frightened and afraid to go to sleep at night. The Attorney-General had no comment to make on the RCMP's investigation of the Flatrock Fires.

This brief article did not tell the whole story. The house in question belonged to a man named Mike Parsons. He had gone to the press with his story, hoping to attract the attention of any research party that might want to look into the matter. He was disappointed when the RCMP and the St. John's Fire Department failed to come up with a satisfactory explanation. Parsons thought some sort of spiritualism was involved. His wife was so upset over it all, that she had become ill. Mrs. Parsons told the press, "I was so frightened that I was laid up in bed, and I had to call the priest in."

The family's troubles began in mid-November. According to Mrs. Parsons, "… we were in the kitchen and smelled smoke. In the woodbox, we found a dictionary burning. There were boughs and dry sticks there, but they were not burning. We were puzzled, but let it go at that."

A few days later, their daughter, Josephine, was in the kitchen with her mother, while her father and uncle were in the barn milking the cows. Josephine told the reporter, "We smelled smoke and started looking around for fire, but couldn't find any. I called out to Dad and Uncle Jim and they came running in to look around."

Mike and Jim found a sack of sugar smoldering in a corner of the kitchen, giving off the sickly odour of burning sugar. "Here's the mysterious thing about it," Mike Parsons told the reporter. "I touched the sugar sack — just touched it with my hand and the fire went out."

The Parsons family gave the reporter a tour of the house, and pointed out the telling evidence of unnatural goings-on. A bureau in an upstairs room had been scarred by burning. This was the result of the sudden immolation of some scared literature. A bedroom that had no electrical wires and no connections to the chimney had mysterious burn marks in the corners. The Parsons could offer no proof about the burning doll, but they swore that their granddaughter's doll had been lying on the kitchen floor when it suddenly burst into flames, as though the fire had come from within it.

There was some speculation that the Parsons family had purposely set the fires for an insurance scam. An RCMP investigation ruled out that possibility. There was no insurance on the property. The basement was filled with their vegetable harvest, and the barn adjacent to the house contained twelve tons of hay, not to mention five sheep, a cow, a calf, and a horse. All this was valuable property that the family certainly could not afford to lose in a fire.

A priest visited the house and blessed it with holy water. An RCMP report was sent to the Department of Justice. The cause of the strange fires remained a mystery. The St. John's *Evening Telegram* stated that similar stories of unexplained fires existed all over the world, and went back hundreds of years. It was concluded that they were the work of poltergeists.

The Whole House Was Haunted

Eileen M. Williamson, who wrote a memoir entitled *Outport: A Newfoundland Journal* (1980), was originally from Regina, Saskatchewan. She wrote about her experiences in the community of Badger; the nearest city is Grand Falls. This story about a haunting experience is not dated, but evidently took place in the 1960s.

I didn't mind working on into the night when Betty was with me, but night after night was spent in my reaction-office room in the basement while John was at organization, club and town council meetings. I hated being alone. Although the house was newly built, it was across the road from the cemetery; there was something very strong about the basement, and indeed I began to think the whole house was haunted. You can't prove ghosts to anyone who has never experienced them and doesn't want to believe in them. You can lead a full, happy and useful life without believing in ghosts — but the people who do give credence to the existence of ghosts are equally intelligent, normal people, many of whom have seen something of the supernatural.

It was one of my pupils who made me realize that I wasn't the only one who sensed something unnatural about the house. He said, "I can't come for any more lessons."

"Why not? You've practically finished the course and you're doing so well."

"I don't like coming here," he answered flatly. "You're too close to the cemetery, and it's dark when I finish my lesson."

I told him that no one in the cemetery would hurt him — and he could come in at the front door which wasn't so close to the cemetery.

"No," he said. "There's something spooky about the house."

I was beginning to think he was right. I'd be trying to write up some event or an article, and all of a sudden I'd have the horrible feeling that I wasn't alone. There was someone or some thing watching me, hiding in the shadows of the big room, or in the rest of the dark basement, perhaps behind the furnace. I'd stop typing to listen. There was a complete stillness — then perhaps I'd hear what sounded like a door quietly closing (although I knew all the doors upstairs were open) or I'd have the illusion that someone was moving about stealthily, a rustle on the floor. Then there would be a horrifying chill in the air. It was a dead, flat cold with sharply defined boundaries, so that if I moved over towards the blazing fire in the fireplace, I was out of it.

I always thought I didn't mind Gremlins — they aren't too frightening, just annoying. I would set up an advertisement, reach for the glue, and find that the illustration I'd been working on and going to stick on the paper wouldn't be there. I'd search on the floor, under papers, and then, not having moved out of my chair, I'd see it on the coffee table across the room. Gremlins seemed just mischievous — but this other thing was really frightening. When that dreadful chill crept over me, I felt I almost had to push my way out of my chair, and run upstairs. And nothing would induce me to go downstairs again to finish my work.

"Don't work down there when you're on your own or if you're nervous. But of course there aren't any ghosts!" John said, and dashed out of his meeting.

On Monday and Thursday nights when my pupils came, their presence seemed to prevent the ghosts romping around.

However, the ghosts didn't altogether confine their activities to the basement.

One evening about 9:30, although there'd been no sign of them for several days, again there was the start of that chill in the air, and the strange atmosphere. I dropped everything and fled upstairs. I grabbed my book, raced for my bedroom and went to bed. And then there was an extraordinary sound — it seemed like a rocking chair, squeakily rocking back and forth, back and forth, occasionally stopping, and then going on again. I sat bolt upright, my hair standing on end, paralyzed with fear, until about midnight John came home.

The next day I told Debbie. Of course she roared with laughter. Then she said, "Why didn't you phone us — we'd have come over!"

"How could I get to the phone," I answered, "with the hall full of ghosts, and that rocking chair?"

We had a guest staying with us for a few days.

"Did you sleep well last night?" I asked her the next morning, as I handed her a plate of bacon and eggs.

"Not too bad," she said, "but did you hear anything in the night?"

"No, what was it?"

"It was the most extraordinary thing. I read for a while after going to bed, then turned out the light. I wakened with the feeling there was someone in the room, and then all of a sudden the light beside my bed blazed on, but no one was there!"

"Oh, — how awful." We stared at one another. "I'm quite sure this house is haunted, but no one believes me, and I didn't think the ghosts would come when you were here. They don't usually when there are strangers around."

"Well, I think the house is haunted. One of the houses we lived in in England was haunted, and there's a definite feeling. I thought this one was as soon as I came in, but I didn't like to say anything to you in case you hadn't noticed anything."

A few weeks later we were sound asleep one night when, about three in the morning, we heard the most awful crash, which literally lifted us out of bed.

John looked over the entire house, even down in the basement, although nothing would have induced me to go down there.

"I can't find anything," he said. "Can't imagine what it was."

The next morning I went into the dining room to put the breakfast on the table.

"There's something missing — oh, there's no picture on the wall."

John came in and we looked behind the buffet. There we discovered the picture, quite a large one, about sixteen by twenty, had fallen. The nail was still in the wall, the glass wasn't broken, although it was quite a drop to the floor for such a large picture, the wire was still intact.

"But surely," I said to John, "that picture falling wouldn't have made such a thunderous noise!"

Debbie had acted as editor for the paper two or three times when we were on holidays. Usually I took everything that I thought she'd need over to her house, so that she could work there, but of course I always left her the key to our place in case she found she needed something I'd forgotten, or in case she wanted to look up something kept in the basement where copies of the old newspapers were stored.

The day after we returned from England, she raced over and said, "You know, you're right — this house really is haunted!"

"What happened?"

"We came over one evening to look up something, and were in the basement when we heard the most tremendous crash upstairs. We tore upstairs and looked in all the rooms, but couldn't find a thing that could have fallen — there was nothing! So we went down to the basement again to pick up our things and turn the lights off — and there was the most awful, icy appalling chill. It was really quite frightening. We sure didn't linger there!"

The climax came one winter afternoon. A howling blizzard was blowing outside, but every light was on in the recreation-office room, a lovely big fire was blazing away in the fireplace, no ghosts had appeared for several weeks, and I was working happily and busily — when I was hit in the face with a snowball!

I jumped at least seven feet straight up. I put my hand on my face — it was wet! On a smaller desk which was used by my typing pupils, and about three feet from my own desk where I was sitting, there was a fairly good-sized snowball, beginning to melt!

I was too petrified to get up and run out of the room, but I had to speak to someone in a hurry — some human voice. I reached for the phone, dialed Debbie's number, and breathed a sigh of relief when she answered immediately.

"The ghosts have just thrown a snowball at me," I said.

There was a roar of laughter, and I joined her a bit shakily. She said, "Did they hit you?"

"Yes — my face is still wet!"

"Did it come through the window — there's an awful wind blowing."

I said, "Even if it did come through the window, I'm not sitting under it — and there's the snowball melting on the typist's desk. And that's about three or four feet away!"

"Well, feel if the window-sill is wet."

I got up, and reaching up to the high basement window, I felt all along the still. It was bone dry.

Just then, to my great relief, I heard a couple of my typing pupils coming up the path to the back door, chatting merrily, so we rang off.

I rushed upstairs to let them in. "I'm so glad to see you," I said. "Come on in. You can both bear witness to the fact that my ghosts have been throwing snowballs at me!"

Somewhat reluctantly, they came downstairs. Both stared at the small lump of snow sitting in a puddle of water.

Their eyes like saucers, one of them breathed, "Lard Jaysus — let's go 'ome!"

"Of course you can't go home — you can't leave me now. Let's go to work."

Briskly I mopped up the snow, and they proceeded with their "hunt and punch" method of thumping the typewriters.

A Near Trip to Heaven

This fascinating story of a Newfoundland haunting appears here courtesy of John Robert Colombo, to whom it was submitted in March 2006. It comes from a Newfoundland-born woman named Holly, who was a resident of Alberta at the time.

It was around early fall and I was around eight or nine years old. Gran, my step-great-grandmother (I call her this because she adopted my grandfather when he was a small boy, and I tell you this because I think it is important to my story) died when I was around four, and I remember the wake vividly, even at such a tender age. Anyway, I was lying in my bed late one night — I found it hard to fall asleep as a child, sometimes not getting to sleep till the wee hours of the morning. I was staring at the ceiling when a strange, shivery feeling came over me. This is strange because in our house the heat was always cranked well above 20 degrees Celsius. I was startled and looked around thinking my window was open. It wasn't. I then noticed a glowing white ball of light above my window. Needless to say, I hauled the covers over my head pretty quickly, and that was the end of that.

A few nights later, after I had turned my bed away from my window, I was visited again by a "shivery" feeling. I opened my eyes and to my horror, there was a woman hovering about a foot off the floor at the end of my bed. She was transparent and had very long grey hair. Her face was sullen and very pale. She was around seventy or eighty years old, wearing a long, plain dress. I couldn't move, I was terrified but I could not look away from her stare. She floated around the foot of my bed to the side. I would say she was no more than a foot away from me. She held out her hand at which time I found the courage to move and pulled the covers over my head, although I was still tongue-tied and couldn't cry out to my parents who were sleeping in the next room.

My fear of this woman returning forced me to sleep with the lights on for several nights after. I wouldn't go into the sleeping area of our house without someone accompanying me, usually my younger brother, who, needless to say, as little boys are, wasn't afraid of anything.

The biggest shock came when some months later, my grandmother came to live with us. I related the ghostly encounter to her. She immediately went pale and stared at me in horror. "The spirit you saw was Gran, and if you would have taken her hand, you surely would have went to heaven with her."

I would also like to add, I've since seen pictures of my Gran and this is without a doubt the woman who visited me that night. I since have no fear of spirits or ghosts and hope someday she will visit again. Hopefully I will not be scared stiff if there be a next time, as I would like to speak with her, if she should choose to speak back.

Oft Told Tales: Labrador

The Mysterious Trapper of Labrador

Many ghost stories are tales of retribution; spooky examples of the old adage, "What goes around, comes around." One of the most familiar ghosts in English literature is that of Jacob Marley in the Charles Dickens classic, *A Christmas Carol.* Because he had been a hard-hearted miser in life, Marley is doomed to wander the earth forever, fettered by his moneyboxes. The story revolves around his attempt to save his old business partner, Ebenezer Scrooge, from the same awful fate. The wilds of Labrador are the stage for a drama with a similar plot involving a wicked life, followed by penitence in the afterlife.

In life, Labrador's most notorious trapper is believed to have been Esau Dillingham, from Newfoundland. Dillingham arrived in Labrador in about 1900, with the intention of making his living as a trapper. He ran trap lines for a year or two, but then quit, either because the fur harvest was poor, or the work was too hard. Dillingham found that he could make more money, and a lot easier, by bootlegging.

Dillingham made his own booze in a backwoods still, and like most homemade firewater, it was a vile brew. Too much of Dillingham's overproof moonshine could result in alcoholic poisoning, blindness, insanity, or even death. He sold it to Natives and to white men who bought it because it was cheaper than legal spirits, and easier to get. Dillingham would bring it right to the customer's cabin, saving him a long trip to a settlement. Because of its high potency, people called Dillingham's rotgut liquor "smoke," earning him the nickname Smoker.

Smoker had a reputation that was as bad as his hooch. He was argumentative and violent, and usually not welcome in the rugged Labrador settlements. Some people said he was a cruel man by nature, but others believed that drinking too much of his own booze had made him crazy. Among the worst of his crimes was rape. Smoker would assault women in lonely cabins while their husbands were out tending their traplines.

Some stories say that Smoker was never apprehended by the law. Others say that he was arrested once, and served a year in jail in St. John's for bootlegging. That, they explain, was the reason for his all-white dogsled. Smoker had a team of fourteen pure white huskies, of which he was exceedingly proud. His sled was painted white, and he wore a parka, pants, and mittens made from snow-white fur. This camouflage made him almost invisible against the snowy landscape of Labrador. Many times the police pursued him, but he always managed to get away. Or so some of the stories claim.

The tales do not agree on how Smoker met his end. One says he died of natural causes in his cabin in the wild. Another says he was shot by the husband of a woman he had assaulted. Yet another claims that he was drunk, and staggering around on a fish flake, when he fell and broke his back. And one more version has it that Smoker was arrested for murder and imprisoned, and that while in jail he took a fall and broke his neck.

The stories all agree, however, that when Smoker realized that he was dying, he suddenly feared eternal damnation. He desperately prayed to be spared the torments of hell. He asked for a chance to keep driving his dog team after death, so that he could make up for the evil way he had lived.

According to the legend of the Trapper's Ghost, Smoker's prayer was answered. Labrador's cold wilderness, where he had lived his life of sin, became his purgatory. Every winter, the Trapper's Ghost roams the land on a sled pulled by white huskies, bound by his pledge to help others. Over the years there have been stories of travellers who got in trouble on Labrador's rugged, lonely trails, who owed their lives to the phantom.

One story is of a a trapper who was caught in a blizzard far from any shelter. The man had almost frozen to death when the Trapper's Ghost appeared from out of the howling storm. The ghost placed the man on the sled, covered him with blankets, and mushed through the driving snow until they reached a settlement. The local hotel keeper saw a stranger come through the door, carrying a man who was barely alive. The stranger put the man in a chair, told the hotel keeper to take care of him, and vanished into thin air.

Another story says that in 1949, the year Newfoundland and Labrador became Canada's tenth province, two RCMP officers unfamiliar with the Labrador trails, became lost in a blizzard while on patrol. They thought they were doomed to an icy death, when they saw a figure dressed in white driving a sled pulled by white huskies. The Mounties followed the sled, thinking the man must be a local trapper who knew the trails and would lead them to safety. After a few hours of cold, hard travelling, the officers arrived at a cabin in which some trappers had taken refuge from the storm. The policemen staggered in, thankful for the warmth of a hot stove and the company of other men. They thought that the man they had been following must be in there, too. But when they enquired about him, they were told that they were the first people to enter the cabin since the storm began. The trappers told the Mounties that they had been saved by the ghost of a man who, in his lifetime, had been an outlaw.

The tales of mysterious rescues continued right up to the early 1970s, when the Trapper's Ghost was said to have led an American schoolteacher to an abandoned hunting lodge when he got lost during a storm. As the teacher opened the door, he turned to thank his guide, but before his eyes the man disappeared in a swirl of snow.

In addition to leading lost travellers to safety, the Trapper's Ghost also made appearances that seemed to be warnings of coming storms, giving people the chance to seek shelter. All that was seen of him was a figure dressed in white, mushing his white huskies across the snow. Anyone who went to investigate found that the sled had left no tracks.

Charles Dickens never told his readers if Jacob Marley, by virtue of his role in the redemption of Ebenezer Scrooge, was at last pardoned for his sins and freed of his chains and money boxes. Nor do we know if Esau Dillingham has paid his moral debt, and moved on along the eternal trail. Or is he still a lonely soul in the wilds of Labrador, looking for yet another traveller in need of a stranger's helping hand?

The Mystery of Sam Croucher's Gold

Not all stories of buried treasure guarded by supernatural forces involve pirates. In isolated communities and frontier regions where there were no banks, people often placed money and other valuables in secret places in order to keep them safe. Sometimes, if a person who had hidden treasure away died without revealing the location to anyone, legends arose about how the site was protected by the ghost of the deceased or some other unearthly manifestation. One such story is that of a man named Sam Croucher.

In the early nineteenth century, Sam Croucher was a salmon fisherman who lived near Stag Point on the coast of Labrador with his wife, an adopted daughter, and a son who was almost blind. Sam prospered at his trade, but he did not trust paper money or any other kind of financial note. He always made sure that the fruits of his labours were realized in gold coins.

As the years passed, Sam accumulated quite a large hoard of gold coins. At first he kept them in a strongbox in his house. Then he began to worry that thieves might break in and rob him. He also feared that in a fire, his precious coins would melt into a lump of gold that would be of less value. Sam decided to bury his life's savings in a secret place.

One morning before dawn he awoke his near-sighted son to help him take his money to a nearby island and bury it. The son helped row the boat, but because of the darkness and his poor eyesight, he did not know where they had landed. Moreover, his father told him to remain in the boat while he went and buried the gold. When Sam came back, he told his son he had marked the site so it would be easy to find. Father and son then rowed back to Stag Point, leaving a small fortune in a location known only to Sam. He did not even tell his wife and daughter, fearing that some outsider might pry the secret out of them.

Sam Croucher died suddenly, taking the secret with him. Stories about his buried hoard spread, and many treasure hunters searched for it. They didn't find a thing. Years passed, and the story was eventually forgotten. Sam's adopted daughter married a man named James T. Morris of Bolsh Rock, Labrador.

One night Mrs. Morris had a strange dream. Her dead father appeared to her, and told her exactly where the gold was buried. It was hers on two conditions; she must go to the treasure site alone, and she had to share the gold with her brother.

Mrs. Morris followed the ghost's instructions. She set off by herself for the island. But she came back empty handed and it was clear that something disturbing had happened to her. She refused to talk about it. She said that nothing could make her go back to look for Sam Croucher's gold. Whatever she had seen, it was just too horrible and frightening.

Could it have been possible that Sam's spirit would play a cruel trick on his daughter? Or was the woman deceived by something that was not Sam at all? As far as anyone knows, Sam Croucher's gold is still buried on an island off the coast of Labrador.

Case Files: Ghosts of Labrador

The Ghosts of Labrador logo.

Matt Massie and Frank Pottle are the founders and moderators of a website called Ghosts of Labrador. This is a forum in which Labrador residents can share their paranormal experiences. The following stories were submitted to Matt and Frank, and appear here with their kind permission.

Courtney's Story: Slamming Doors

When we first moved over to Wabush, it was about a month after we had moved there that my mom decided to go grocery shopping. I was home alone because my brother was over to his friend's all day, and my sister had gone out as well. I was upstairs in my room, and my mother called out to me to let me know she was going.

Once she had left, I went down in the living room and began watching television. After about twenty minutes, I heard a door slam upstairs, which made me jump. I assumed someone must have left a window open and the wind pushed the door shut. Continuing to watch my TV show, I heard the door slam again upstairs, and at this point it was getting annoying. So I ran upstairs to close the window, and stop the door from hitting back and forth once and for all.

When I got to the top of the stairs both my brother and sister's doors were closed. The three other doors were open all the way. Clearly I thought, *Grrr! Stupid Catherine and Adam, forgetting to close their windows.*

So I opened my sister's door and the window was closed. It must be Adam's room, but when I went to open the door, his window was also shut. By this time my heart was pounding and I was getting a little scared, but reassured myself there had to be a window open in one of the rooms. After my search came up clean, I ran downstairs and sat cross-legged on the couch. Five minutes passed, and all I heard was *bang, bang, bang*, and I could hear someone running up and down the hall. I yelled out, "Catherine, Adam, whichever one of you is doing this, I am telling Mom when she gets home."

At this point I was in tears, and picked up the phone to call my sister Nicole, and when she answered I was crying about how Catherine or Adam were messing with me. She told me that it would be okay and to tell Mom when she got home. The doors slamming and someone running up and down the hall kept going for another ten minutes, at least. I heard my Mom pull up in the driveway, got off the phone with my sister, and ran out the door in tears, freaking out to my mom how someone was trying to scare me.

As I ran out to tell her, my brother was coming up the street, and Catherine was pulling in the driveway with one of her friends. *What the eff?* I thought. My mom said it was okay, and gave me the whole Mom Talk. Catherine and Adam just laughed at me. I have no idea what it was, but it was years before I stayed alone in that house. Even today when I am alone in that house, I will not leave the room to venture anywhere else because I don't want to ever relive that day.

Jenny's Story: The Man Behind the Furnace

It happened in my own house in Labrador City, not too far from the Indian Point playground. Before I tell you my story, I have to explain the layout of my basement. There is a huge rec room, and then connected to that is a storage room. The storage room is where the furnace, washer and dryer, and some old boxes and junk are, basically. But in between the rec room and the storage room (or, as we call it, the back room), there's the stairs that leads to the upstairs of my house. This is the only exit from the basement.

It was winter time, and I was twelve years old. Me and one of my closest friends had just gotten home from school. We decided to come to my house and watch TV in the basement like we usually did. As we were coming in the door, my mom asked me to watch my twin brothers for an hour because she had to run to the grocery store. After she left, me and my friend went down in my basement to watch my brothers, who were only five years old.

So we turned on the television, and my brothers started riding around on their tricycles as they normally did. That was annoying to us at the time, because they used to ride in front of the TV so that whatever we were watching would have to be interrupted every time they passed in front of us. This went on for about half an hour, when I noticed that we were no longer being interrupted. Things got very quiet. The first thought that came to my mind was that they had gotten into a fight and one of them was hurt, but they were too scared to come and tell me.

That was when I saw my two brothers come running as fast as they could out of the back room with tears pouring down their shaking bodies. I tried to sit them down and ask them what was wrong, but they were crying too much to get it out. When they finally calmed down, one of them spoke up and said, "The man behind the furnace took my bike."

When I heard these words, my heart sank into my stomach, as I was just as scared as they were. We all curled up on the couch, afraid to run upstairs in case the man would grab us on the way. It was about fifteen minutes later when my stepdad arrived home. He rushed downstairs because he heard us screaming. When he came down, we told him what had happened. He started to make his way into the back room when he saw one of the tricycles by the furnace. He kept walking until he got behind the furnace where he saw the other tricycle bent up in ways that seemed impossible for him to do with his own two hands.

This, of course, startled my stepdad, so he started looking for the man who might have done this. But no man ever did show up. We were sitting on the couch the whole time, so we would have seen the man go up the stairs, which was the only exit out of the basement, because all the windows were buried in with snow. To this day, we do not know where the man came from or where he went. It is still a mystery.

About a year later, my mother was sleeping in her bed, when she heard her bedroom door open. She sat up, figuring that it was one of my little brothers, but standing at the edge of her bed was a little girl. My mom said it didn't look like a ghost, it looked like an actual little girl. So she turned around to wake up my stepdad, and when she did her bedroom door slammed shut and the little girl was no longer there. She got my stepdad out of bed and made him search the whole house. He woke me and my brothers up to check in our closets and under our beds. He went up in the attic, and down behind the furnace where the last incident had happened. He checked everywhere he possibly could check, but there was no sign of that little girl. We figured that she might have left the house so we opened up the two doors that lead to the outside of our house, but it was all freshly fallen snow, and no sign of any footprints ever being there. Where had the little girl gone? No one will ever know.

Amanda's Story: Indian Graves

When I was about seven years old we lived in one of the town houses on Tamarack by the Indian Point playground. Rumour has it that the houses were built over Indian graves. I remember my sister always hated going into the basement, but I always told her she was being foolish. For a long time I didn't hear anything, see anything, nothing.

Then when I was twelve, I was up in my room hanging out. My mom called out to say she was going out. My stepdad and my sister had already gone out, so I was there alone.

I heard a woman singing, quietly at first, then getting a little louder. It was in a different language, but I still remember the tune and melody of it to this day. I figured it was my mom. She loves to sing. I went downstairs. "Mom, you home?" Nothing. She walked in the door a dew minutes later. I asked her if she had just gotten home, and told her what I heard. She said I was crazy and laughed it off. But I know what I heard.

Some few years later I met Clive H. He told me a story of how he used to live in one of those houses and was once pushed down the basement stairs by a ghost. We have determined it was the same house.

I have met another woman who once stayed in my old bedroom in that same house overnight. She said that when she sat down on her bed, she saw a bum print sit down next to her. She said she had a conversation with an old man.

Pamela's Story: "This is Really Beginning to Scare Me"

My family and I moved into this trailer home almost two years ago and since then we have had three unexplainable things happen to us. Plus, our daughter has told me on one occasion that she had seen a ghost. While telling me this she was pointing out where it was, and the cat was on a chair hissing and trying to attack something in that very same spot.

The first unexplainable thing that happened to me was when I had a couple of friends over, and they stayed pretty late. We were just chatting away when we heard a noise, like something had fallen, and sure enough when we went to check to see what the noise was, the butter knife that I had placed on top of the butter dish was at least four metres away from where I had put it. And the strange thing is that it also had to move around an object to get where it landed. It had to fly around a wall!

The second unexplainable thing happened to my spouse and his two friends, and again this was a little late at night. They were all watching the movie *The Hills Have Eyes*, and they all said that while watching the movie, our son's remote control truck moved forward really fast, and then back into the spot it had left really slow. The remote for the truck was near one of my spouse's friends, and he had not touched it.

The third unexplainable thing that happened was just last night. I was playing around in the dark, keeping an eye on my spouse. I was trying to give him a fright. Then I heard this sound, and my spouse heard it, too. It was the sound of a small, round object rolling on the floor. I was still in the dark area when I heard this, and it sounded like it was right by me. Then I got this real ugly feeling like someone was there. I ran into the living room where my spouse was and told him about the noise. He said he had heard it, too, and he tried to pass it off as the cat playing around. I then proved to him that the cat was under the arm chair. I said it sounded like a marble rolling around. He went to look around, and found nothing but a piece of paper. But when he went back to the kitchen moments after, he raised his hand in the air and showed me a marble. Remember, it wasn't there when he first checked. This is really beginning to scare me, and I was a non-believer.

Olive's Story: "I Could See Right Through Him"

I remember this one clearly because it scared the shiz out of me, and it takes a lot to scare me, but I totally believe in ghosts. I was at my uncle's cabin with him and my cousins. We used to go down every weekend we could, and they had always told me stories of a ghost at the cabin, but I never believed them. I thought they were just trying to scare me because we were like, thirteen and fourteen.

One day we were at the cabin and I decided to go for a walk. They wouldn't come with me; they were playing cards. I was all by myself, and was a nice ways away from the cabin in deep woods, but I was walking on a small narrow trail, an old trapping trail. As I was walking, I heard something in the trees a few feet away. I looked over and thought I saw my cousin Max. It looked just like him. I began to yell at him, "Max, what are you doing?" With no response from him I yelled again, louder, "Max, come here you little brat, stop playing around. I know you hear me."

To my surprise he finally looked at me, but with the most weakening feeling over my whole body ever, I realized it looked like him alright, but I could see right through him. I could see the trees behind him. You see, my cousin Max is still alive, he's not dead. That's what makes this so scary.

I stood puzzled and shocked for what seemed like a couple of minutes. I yelled again, "Max, is that you?"

He looked at me walking slowly through the trees. Then it hit me full force; it wasn't really Max, it was a ghost! I turned to start running back to the cabin, screaming as loud as I could, running as fast as I could. It felt like I was running slow, and I kept telling myself to run faster. I realized that I was running as fast as I could, but being so scared and weak in my mind, it felt like I was going slow. I could feel my knees getting weaker and weaker. I would see a stump or tree knocked down, and tell myself to jump over it, but I would trip instead. I guess because I was so scared.

Finally reaching the cabin, as I was running by the side of it, I began hitting the wall all down the side of it, screaming till I reached the front door. I ran into the cabin and almost died when I sat on the chair, from being beat out.

The girls looked at me. "What's wrong?" they said. I told them what had happened. They said nothing but looked at each other with a scared look. I wondered why they weren't laughing at me or surprised.

"Olive, Dad saw the same, and me too. He looked just like him, eh?" said my cousin. I swear I could have fainted. This is the single most scary thing ever to happen to me — in the ghost sense. This took place at my uncle's cabin at the mouth of the Goose River. I have heard my uncles tell many scary stories of seeing a ghost there.

Cherie's Story: Try to Explain That

Ten years ago, my husband and I lived in a two storey house in Goose Bay with our seventeen-month-old son. There were three bedrooms upstairs.

Two of the bedrooms were very comfortable, but there was something very different about my son's bedroom and he was terrified to sleep in it. When placed in his crib to sleep, he would awake in a cold sweat, and his cry was so different than a normal cry as he would point at the closet. Because of his fears, we had to move his crib into our bedroom.

One evening my husband went to work, and I was vacuuming downstairs. I could hear a baby crying upstairs. I went upstairs to check on my son, who was asleep in my bedroom, to find that he was still asleep. I checked in all of the bedrooms, and nothing was out of the ordinary.

I went back downstairs to vacuum again, and the cries continued to get louder. So I went back upstairs to see what was going on. My son was still sleeping in my room, but when I walked into his room, the window screen had been removed from the window and placed on the bed, which was on the opposite side of the room, and his window was wide open. Just remember, I was up there a few minutes earlier, and nothing was out of the ordinary. Try to explain that one.

Jennifer's Story: A Big Bang

I lived in a house on Cavendish Crescent about five years ago, and it was the freakiest experience of my life. Every night at about 12:00 a.m. I would hear a big bang come from upstairs, and I would be the only person in the house. So then my neighbour came over one day and asked me what the hell was going on every night. I asked her what she meant, and she said that a big bang wakes her every night, because it's right next to her bedroom.

I knew then that something was wrong. I told her the problem, and she said that was freaky shit. Every time it happened, I went upstairs, and nothing had fallen or was out of place. Also, in that same house, I was home alone one night, and I was upstairs in my bedroom, and I heard footsteps coming up the wooden stairs and down the hallway and stop at my door. I crept out the door, and there was no one there.

Now the freaky part is that while I heard footsteps coming down the hall, I clearly heard a man swearing and muttering under his breath. We had a lot of scary experiences in that house.

Jody's Story: I Hate That House

I'll tell you about the scariest house ever. I hate that house ... I mean, really hate it. My friend was living there a few years, and we always heard things like footsteps, people talking, and dishes moving. It was not always in the night time. Most of it happened in the daylight, and that creeped me out even more, for some reason. I always felt something when I went in that house, and so did my friend. The longer she was in that house, the more unexplained things happened.

One evening after supper, she called me, totally freaked out and said that "something" had pushed her head into the corner of the wall. When I arrived at her house, I saw her holding her head, and you could see the pain she was in. This was the start of it.

I slept at her house more that year than I slept at home. While I was staying there, she had to stay close to the washroom while I got in the shower. Silly, I know, but I thought that was the creepiest place in the house. I even used to keep the curtain open a bit because I just knew something was watching and waiting for the perfect chance to scare the crap out of me. We always went to bed at the same time, and the two if us used to meet up in the middle of the hallway to say, "Did you hear that?" not minutes after hitting the hay.

I saw the same "man" standing by her front door three different times. It was almost like the guy from the *Blair Witch*, the one who is facing the wall at the end. It used to scare me to tears. He used to just stand there, always when it was time for me to go. I then started going out the side door, running. The last time, he made for sure it was a good one.

My friend and I were standing in her porch, and bent over putting our shoes on, when we heard the loudest, scariest, most terrifying roar. She pushed me out of the way, grabbed her keys, and ran screaming out of the house. We stood two feet from her front step, looking in, for what seemed forever. My friend and I were frozen. When we finally broke, so did the tears. "We have to go, we have to go!" she said. She reached in her pocket for her keys, but they were not there. We thought they fell on the ground. We looked everywhere, but we could not find them.

I looked in through the door, and almost cried again. They were on her key rack. The two of us knew she took them. *Knew*! It took us forever and a day to go in there and get them. When we finally got them, we drove to my house and stayed up the whole night telling my mother what happened. When we decided to go back the next morning, we brought a friend and a crowbar with us. We searched the house, and nothing. There was never anything. We hardly speak of it now. It still gives me the creeps. I hope the people who live in that house now are not experiencing what we did, and I hope they sleep better than I did. It took me a long time not to think of it every time I closed my eyes. I *hate* that house!

Matt's Story: "I Got a Little Freaked"

When my parents were away for the summer last year, I was alone in the house and playing piano. All of a sudden I heard some light footsteps. They sounded like the person weighed about the size of a small child. Anyways, when I stopped playing piano to listen, I couldn't hear them anymore. So I got a little freaked out, and my first thought was it's either Luckey (my dog) or a robber. So I grabbed something off the piano, something heavy that I could attack the robber with, and I started creeping around the corner. I checked the entire house, and there was no one. When I was checking the kitchen, I glanced outside and saw Luckey tied to his doghouse. But there was no one to be found in the house, so I figured I was probably just insane and hearing things. So I went back to playing piano.

Again I heard the footsteps, so I stopped playing. This is the worst part. While I was listening and still not playing the piano, I heard them again. Crystal clear. The house was dead silent, except for the footsteps walking around out in the kitchen. I would hear them, then it would seem like whatever it was would pause, and then keep walking. So I almost fainted and left the house for a few hours.

Frank and I were driving home from Northwest River at night. We were about halfway between NWR and Gosling Park, when up ahead, about a hundred feet, we saw a light. It was between the size of a softball and a soccer ball, slightly bluish tinged. It floated up about three or four feet off the ground, and floated across the road until it got halfway, then it disappeared. No idea what it was.

This is the second part to this story. Three days ago, Chris, Frank, and I were driving around up by Chris's brother's house, and we were heading towards the end of the road that branched off into two dirt trails. I didn't want to take them in my car, so I stopped to turn around. As the headlights passed over the trail, Frank and I (who were in the front) saw a shape move across the path. We both saw it as a shape, and about the size of a medium dog, but with no definite shape (i.e. legs, head, tail). It looked to be basically an oval, and it was *pure black*! There was no reflection whatsoever; not from shiny fur, from eyes, nothing. It was just a black shape, like a shadow, but it moved in the air across the path, from one side to the other, into the woods. I realized the next day that we had seen two completely unexplained things; one pure light, the other pure dark. Weird!

Odd Tales

A Problematic Dream

Can people control what they dream? Cromwell F. Varley was a British-born engineer working in Newfoundland. In 1860 he experienced what he called "a problematic dream" while staying at Harbour Grace. This account is taken from the interesting collection called *Noted Witnesses for Psychic Occurrences* by Walter Franklin Prince, a psychologist and psychical researcher. His book is an annotated anthology of more than 170 experiences of a "spontaneous" nature. His book was published by the Boston Society for Psychical Research in 1928.

"This incident was told by Mr. Varley, a prominent English electrician, to the London Dialectical Society," wrote Prince, who cited *Report on Spiritualism of the Committee of the London Dialectical Society* (London, 1873). Prince went on to discuss the curious characteristics of this dream, which he considered to be "problematic." Here is Varley's account of the dream.

> I have had another case in 1860; I went to find the first Atlantic Cable; when I arrived at Halifax, my name was telegraphed to New York. Mr. Cyrus Field telegraphed the fact to St. John's and then to Harbour Grace; so that when I arrived I was very cordially received at each place, and at Harbour Grace found there was a supper prepared. Some speeches followed and we sat up late.

I had to catch the steamer that went early the next morning and was fearful of not waking in time, but I employed a plan which had often proved successful before, viz., that of willing strongly that I should wake at the proper time. Morning came and I saw myself in bed asleep; I tried to wake myself, but could not. After a while I found myself hunting about for some means of more power, when I saw a yard in which was a large stack of timber and two men approaching; they ascended the stack of timber and lifted a heavy plank. It occurred to me to make my body dream that there was a bombshell thrown in front of me which was fizzing at the touchhole, and when the men threw the plank down I made my body dream that the bomb had burst and cut open my face. It woke me, but with a clear recollection of the two actions — one, the intelligent mind acting upon the brain in the body, which could be made to believe any ridiculous impression that the former produced by will power. I did not allow a second to elapse before I leapt out of bed, opened the window, and there were the yard, the timber, and the two men, just as my spirit had seen them. I had no previous knowledge at all of the locality; it was dark the previous evening when I entered the town, and I did not even know there was a yard there at all. It was evident I had seen these things while my body lay asleep. I could not see the timber until the window had been opened.

The following essay is Walter Franklin Prince's scientific observation concerning Varley's account.

This is one of the most interesting dreams for study with which I am acquainted. On the one hand it is easy to form a theory of normal explanation. While dreaming he heard the sound, correctly guessed that it was caused by a falling plank, inferred that therefore there was probably a yard near the house containing timber, also inferred from the sound that the plank must be too heavy to be lifted by one man, and correctly guessed that there were two. All this, although a happy combination of accurate inferences and guesses, might be possible. But Mr. Varley testifies that he dreamed he saw a stack of timber and two men approach, ascend the stack and lift the plank, and that he dreamed a devise to make himself wake, before he had the sensation of noise in the dream. An ordinary person might during the time which had elapsed since the dream, nine years, have misplaced the order of its details, but it is less likely that a man of science strongly impressed and bound to study his recollections on waking, should have done so. But there is some evidence tending to show that dreams affected by real sensory impressions do sometimes rearrange the time order so as to present on waking the illusion that the cause of the sensory impression was imagined before the impression itself was received. But it is at least exceedingly rare that a dream should present imagery corresponding to the real facts, as though by inferences, and yet not connect that imagery at all with the sensory impression as its cause, but attribute the cause to something entirely different. Mr. Varley's dream correctly pictured the real external facts, yard, stack of timber, two men, plank and fall of plank, but ascribed the sound to a bomb! If "clairvoyance," whatever process that term really covers, is deemed established by a mass of other evidence, it is perhaps simpler to ascribe this particular case to it.

Varley's sleeping vision intrigued another researcher. Several of Varley's experiences were reproduced in an abridged form by Leslie Shepard in the first volume of his monumental work *Encyclopedia of*

Occultism and Parapsychology (1979). Shepard noted that Varley seemed able to bring about "the liberation of the double in the state of sleep ..."

Scared to Death

This story was kindly contributed by John Robert Columbo and may well be regarded as an instance of a self-fulfilling prophecy. Either that or it is a testimony to the power of a curse. It originally appeared as a letter in the correspondence column of the British Medical Journal, No. 5,457, August 7, 1965. It concerns the death of a woman following routine surgery at North West River Hospital, Labrador.

Founded in 1915 by the International Grenfell Association, the hospital was located at North West River, northeast of Goose Bay, Labrador. It has since been closed.

I am pleased to be able to offer this account to my readers, verbatim. I am also relieved to be able to do so because the story has haunted me for some time. I first read about it in *Arthur C. Clarke's World of Strange Powers* (London: Collins, 1984). Written by John Fairley and Simon Welfare, the book that served as the basis of the popular Yorkshire television series of the same name; one of the few programs on television that seriously considered claims of the supernatural and the paranormal, and regarding it both sympathetically and unsensationally.

Scared to Death

SIR, —We would like to report a case of an apparently healthy middle-aged woman dying with massive adrenal haemorrhage, following a relatively minor operation, who was subsequently found to have had forebodings of death.

Mrs. A.B., aged 43, mother of five children, was admitted to North West River Hospital, Labrador, on 18 March 1965. She had been complaining of severe stress incontinence for several months. She had been treated during the past three years for anxiety which

208

responded well to reassurance and mild sedation with phenobarbitone, 30 mg., three times daily. There was no relevant past medical history. On examination she was found to be in good health. Vaginal examination revealed a moderately large cystocele and urethrocele. On 19 March anterior colporrhaphy was performed under general anaesthesia. The premedication was pathidine, 100 mg., and atropine, 0.65 mg.; induction with intravenous thiopentone, 400 mg., and Flaxedil (gallamine triethiodide), 40 mg.; maintenance with nitrous oxide, oxygen, and a trace of trilene, accompanied by intermittent intravenous pethidine to a total of 80 mg. The operation, which lasted less than one hour, was straightforward with minimal blood loss. Her blood pressure remained around 120/70 throughout the operation, and pulse and respiration were normal. She regained consciousness before leaving the theatre. One hour later she became shocked and her systolic blood-pressure fell to 70 mm. Hg. She remained conscious, but shortly afterwards complained of severe pain in the left hypochondrium. Methedrine (methylamphetamine) was immediately given, 15 mg. intravenously, and 15 mg. intramuscularly, and the foot of the bed was raised. As the blood pressure showed no response Aramine (metaraminol), 10 mg., was given intramuscularly. An infusion of dextran, 500 ml., with hydrocortisone, 100 mg., was started. Despite continuous infusion with metaraminol and hydrocortisone no improvement was obtained and intranasal oxygen was required as the patient became cyanosed. The pain was partly controlled by injections of morphone, 16 mg., given on three occasions. The E.C.G. was normal. Her condition deteriorated and her temperature rose to 103.6° F. (39.8° C.) by midnight, when she became comatose. She died at 5 a.m. on 20 March.

At post-mortem examination the adrenal glands showed extensive haemorrhage. Petachial haemorrhages were found in the stomach, ileum, liver, and in the skin of the nose. There was no other pathology.

Subsequently we learned that this patient had had her fortune told at the age of 5 years, when she was informed that she would die when she was 43 years old. She had told her daughter for many years that she would die at this age. Her forty-third birthday was one week before operation. On the evening before operation she told her sister, who alone knew of the prophecy, that she did not expect to awake from the anaesthetic, and on the morning of operation the patient told a nurse she was sure she was going to die. These fears were not known to us at the time of operation.

We would be grateful to hear from any reader who has had experience of a patient dying under similar circumstances. We wonder if the severe emotional tensions of this patient superimposed on the physiological stress of surgery had any bearing upon her death.—We are, etc.,

A.R. Elkington.
P.R. Steele.
D.D. Yun.
Grenfell Labrador Medical Mission,
Ottawa, Canada

The physicians who signed the letter appealed to "any reader who has had experience of a patient dying under similar circumstances."

Two replies were published in No. 5,461, September 4, 1965. The first was contributed by J.C. Barker of Shelton Hospital, Shrewsbury, Shropshire, England. Barker noted that "one is left wondering why a fortune-teller should impart such devastating information to so young a child which was to make such a terrible and lasting impression upon her." He wondered whether "it is possible that were she a hysterical manipulative type her psychological symptoms, stress incontinence and reaction to it, leading to surgery and its attendant complications, might have resulted from her own unconscious efforts to predetermine her demise at the appointed time, having reflected endlessly upon the admonitions of her soothsayer." He concluded, "Perhaps the boundaries of western psychiatry should now begin to be extended to include some of the phenomena of extra-sensory perception."

The second reply came from A. Fry, of London. He noted that "the case may represent a version of voodoo death." He observed, "A persistent state of fear can end the life of man," and then drew attention to the influence of a persistent state of fear on the sympathetic nervous system and its role in the control of the patient's blood supply. He concluded, "'Scared to Death' is not an idle saying. A feeling 'I am afraid I am going to die' may actually result in death. The anxiety is not removed even when the patient is anaesthetized. Although asleep, the patient is still suffering from anxiety."

In their book Fairley and Welfare concluded intelligently:

> It may be remembered in this connection that fear serves biologically as a defence mechanism which, among other effects, leads to an enhanced activity of the adrenalin glands.... The surgeons in the above case drew the conclusion that death was likely to have resulted indirectly from the stress created by the prophecy. While the present case hopefully involves a reaction of exceptional severity, the self-fulfilling pressure on those who profoundly believe in the fortune-tellers' powers is probably far from negligible; and the number of predictions that have been made to come true in this manner no doubt continue to swell the number of adherents.

Dead Men Can Advance No Farther

Places in which large numbers of people lost their lives in one violent, cataclysmic event are often the sites of hauntings. Old battlefields are prime ground for paranormal activity. Some paranormal researchers have hypothesized that the ground on which battles were fought could have been saturated not only with blood, but also with the powerful emotions and cosmic energies of the combatants who struggled and died there. Some people even consider some soil types to be more sensitive to this phenomenon than others.

Of course, some of the ghostly experiences people have had on historic battlefields may be due to the visitors' own expectations. They have been told the place is haunted, and so they "hear" and even "see" things that they cannot explain. But there are also numerous accounts of battlefield tourists who have been unexpectedly startled by mysterious sights and sounds.

Some investigators believe that battlefields are haunted by the spirits of soldiers who died so suddenly and violently that they don't know that they're dead, so they linger. Others feel that the hauntings are residual; a constant replay of terrifying moments experienced by men in the heat of battle. Such hauntings might fade over time, or they might remain for centuries.

One classic example of a North American battlefield that is allegedly haunted by the ghosts of soldiers long dead is Gettysburg, Pennsylvania, site of the pivotal clash in the American Civil War. Another one is Lundy's Lane, near Niagara Falls, Ontario; the scene of the bloodiest battle in the War of 1812. Newfoundland, too, has historic battle sites; reminders of the days when the French and English tried to blast each other off the island. However, the battleground that was most thoroughly and infamously soaked with the blood of Newfoundlanders, and considered to be one of the most haunted battlefields in the world, is not in Newfoundland, but France. To understand the significance of this particular battlefield to Newfoundlanders, and why even today unsuspecting visitors can be stricken with an overwhelming sense of dread and sorrow, one requires an outline of what happened there.

During the First World War, the men of the Newfoundland Regiment distinguished themselves in several campaigns. But it was on July 1, 1916, the opening day of the Battle of the Somme, that the Newfoundlanders

The Rooms Provincial Archives of Newfoundland and Labrador.

Men of the Newfoundland Regiment embark from St. John's for the battlefields of the Great War. Few of them would return home.

participated in the action for which they are best remembered: the heroic but doomed assault on the German position at Beaumont-Hamel. The events of that day encapsulated the horror and pathos of that war, the courage of the common soldiers, and the folly of the generals — "lions led by donkeys," as a German officer allegedly put it — as well as the willingness of the Allied High Command to fight a war of attrition, taking huge numbers of casualties for small gains.

The Newfoundland Regiment was with the 29th British Division in what was intended to be a push to smash through the heavily fortified German lines and break the stalemate of trench warfare on the Western Front. It began with an artillery bombardment and the detonation of the Hawthorn Mine: 40,000 pounds of dynamite that tunnelers had placed under a key point in the German fortifications. The massive explosion obliterated a large section of the enemy defensive works and created a gap the Allies hoped to exploit. But faulty planning, poor communications, and the speed with which the Germans recovered from the initial blow turned the attack into a debacle.

The men of the Newfoundland Regiment had been well trained. They were confident and their morale was high as they waited in a support trench called St. John's Road for the signal to advance. Two nights earlier, Private Frank Lind had written in a letter, "Tell all friends that the 1st Newfoundland is O.K. and never feels downhearted. We will make you all proud of us someday." This would be Private Lind's last letter home.

The first wave of attacking British troops was mowed down by artillery, rifle, and machine-gun fire. Back in divisional headquarters the commanding officer, Major General Beauvoir De Lisle, mistakenly believed that the German lines had been breached. He gave orders for more troops to be sent to support the attack. The Newfoundland Regiment was with this second wave.

The Newfoundlanders could not move from St. John's Road to the forward lines through communications trenches, because those trenches were under heavy fire and were clogged with dead and wounded men. Their commander, Lieutenant Colonel Arthur Lovell Hadow, decided that the men would have to climb up to the surface and make formation for an attack across open ground. This they did, even though it exposed them to enemy fire while they were still behind the British front line.

It was about 9:15 a.m.

Other British units had either been cut to pieces, or were pinned down by enemy fire. That left the Newfoundlanders as the only soldiers visibly moving on the field. They had to cover 750 yards with no support on their flanks. Each man was burdened with 65 pounds of equipment. They had to thread their way through their own barbed wire before they could cross No Man's Land to strike the German lines. The German machine gunners quickly realized that they could kill the Newfoundlanders by the score if they concentrated their fire on the gaps in the barbed wire that the men had to pass through.

The Germans laid down a withering fire. One observer wrote, "The only visible sign that the men knew they were under this terrific fire, was that they all instinctively tucked their chins into an advanced shoulder as they had so often done when fighting their way home against a blizzard in some little outport in far-off Newfoundland."

This blizzard, however, was one of bullets. The men pressed on, even as their mates fell around them. Many were hit near a solitary tree the Newfoundlanders had named the Danger Tree. It helped German gunners get a fix on their range. A few Newfoundlanders — very few

Photo by R. Cochius.

The Danger Tree on the Second World War battlefield at the Somme, said to be one of the most haunted battlefields in Europe. The Newfoundland Regiment was almost annihilated at the Somme, and many of the soldiers fell near this tree, which the German gunners used to get the range for their deadly fire.

— got close enough to the German trenches to throw their hand-held bombs at the enemy before they, too, were shot down.

In just over half an hour the Newfoundland Regiment was practically annihilated. Of the 810 men who made the advance that morning, only sixty-eight were able to answer roll call the next day. The rest, including every single officer, were dead, wounded, or missing. General De Lisle was quoted as saying, "It was a magnificent display of trained and disciplined valour, and its assault only failed of success because dead men can advance no farther."

In recognition of the Newfoundland Regiment's great sacrifice, the word "Royal" was added to its name. July 1 is Memorial Day in Newfoundland. In France, the 80 acre Newfoundland Memorial Park honours the fallen soldiers. The ground was purchased with funds raised by "the Government and Women of Newfoundland." The old trench system has been preserved, and a statue of a caribou bellowing in anguish dominates the park. Three bronze plaques bear the names of Newfoundlanders who died in action but have no known graves. The crater from the Hawthorn Mine can still be seen, and the petrified

Danger Tree still stands as a stark monument to the men who died around it.

There is something else in that place that was hell-on-earth for the Newfoundland soldiers on that July morning; something not as tangible as the broken ground or the skeletal tree, but essentially just as real. People who have walked across the historic battlefield, even on a warm summer afternoon, have experienced a distinct chill; not the sort that comes from a fresh breeze, but something that reaches right to the bone. They have felt an overwhelming sense of dread and depression, and a sudden urge to get away from the place as quickly as possible. They describe strong feelings of fear and sorrow. Did those unpleasant emotional reactions come from the pre-knowledge of what had happened at that place? Perhaps.

But as has been the case with other battlefield "experiences" among tourists, some of the "spooked" visitors had no more than a rudimentary knowledge of the history of the place. It could be that these people were somehow touched by the shades, emotions, energies, or whatever one may wish to call them, of the slaughtered men of the Newfoundland Regiment.

Bibliography

Butts, Ed. *True Canadian Disaster Stories.* Toronto:Prospero Books, 2006.

Butts, Ed and Harold Horwood. *Pirates & Outlaws of Canada, 1610 – 1932.* Toronto: Doubleday Canada, 1984.

Clery, Val. *Ghost Stories of Canada.* Toronto: Hounslow Press, 1988.

Colombo, John Robert. *Ghosts Galore.* Toronto: Colombo & Company, 1994.

_____. *Mysterious Canada.* Toronto: Colombo & Company, 1998.

_____. *Ghost Stories of Canada.* Toronto: Dundurn Press, 2000.

_____. *True Canadian Ghost Stories.* Toronto: Prospero Books, 2003.

_____. *More True Canadian Ghost Stories.* Toronto: Prospero Books, 2005.

_____. *Strange but True.* Toronto: Dundurn Press, 2007.

_____. *The Big Book of Canadian Ghost Stories.* Toronto: Dundurn Press, 2008.

_____. *The Big Book of Canadian Hauntings.* Toronto: Dundurn Press, 2009.

Fitzgerald, Jack. *Strange But True Newfoundland Stories.* St. Johns, NL: Creative Publishers, 1989.

_____. *Ghosts, Heroes, and Oddities.* St. John's, NL: Jesperson Press, 1991.

_____. *The Hangman is Never Late.* St. John's, NL: Creative Publishers, 1999.

_____. *Ten Steps to the Gallows.* St. John's, NL: Creative Publishers, 2006.

Fowke, Edith. *Legends Told In Canada.* Toronto: Royal Ontario Museum, 1994.

Galgay, Frank and Michael McCarthy. *Buried Treasures of Newfoundland and Labrador.* St. John's, NL: Harry Cuff Publications, 1989.

Guiley, Rosemary Ellen. *The Encyclopedia of Ghosts and Spirits*. New York: Facts On File Inc., 1992.

Halpert, Herbert and J.D.A. Widdowson. *Folktales of Newfoundland*. New York and London: Garland Publishing Inc., 1996.

Hancock, Pat. *Haunted Canada*. Markham, ON: Scholastic Canada, 2003.

_____. *Haunted Canada 2*, Markham, ON: Scholastic Canada, 2005.

Hufford, David J. *The Terror That Comes in the Night*. Philadelphia: University of Pennsylvania Press, 1982.

Jarvis, Dale. *Haunted Shores: True Ghost Stories of Newfoundland and Labrador*. St. John's, NL: Flanker Press2004.

_____. *Wonderful Strange: Ghosts, Fairies, and Wonderful Beasties*. St. John's, NL: Flanker Press, 2005.

O'Neill, Paul. *The Oldest City: The Story of St. John's, Newfoundland*. Erin, ON: Press Porcepic, 1975.

_____. *A Seaport Legacy: The Story of St. John's, Newfoundland*. Erin, ON: Press Porcepic, 1976.

Smallwood, Joseph R. *The Book of Newfoundland*. St. John's, NL: Newfoundland Book Publishers Ltd., 1937–1975.

Steiger, Brad. *Real Ghosts, Restless Spirits, and Haunted Places*. Canton, MI: Visible Ink Press, 2003.

Of Related Interest

Ghost Stories of Saskatchewan 3
by Jo-Anne Christensen
978-1-55488-428-5
$22.99

Saskatchewan and ghost stories. They go together like a grinning scarecrow in a whisper-dry October field. In 1995, Dundurn successfully published *Ghost Stories of Saskatchewan*. Since that time, an eerie wealth of supernatural accounts have surfaced in this seemingly quiet prairie province. In this third collection, a quiet cemetery appears to be a portal between the worlds of the living and the dead, a Victorian mansion-turned-restaurant in Moose Jaw remains occupied by the spectral image of the original lady of the house, and a weary traveller near Flaxcombe stops for coffee in a diner that burned to the ground a decade earlier. Here the reader will find triple the history, mystery, and chills from one of Canada's established authors in the paranormal genre.

DUNDURN PRESS
www.dundurn.com

What did you think of this book?
Visit www.dundurn.com for reviews, videos, updates, and more!

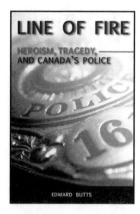

Line of Fire
Heroism, Tragedy, and Canada's Police
978-1-55488-391-2
$24.99

Across Canada peace officers put their lives on the line every day. From John Fisk in 1804, the first known Canadian policeman killed in the line of duty, to the four RCMP officers shot to death in Mayerthorpe, Alberta, in 2005, *Line of Fire* takes a hard-hitting, compassionate, probing look at some of the stories involving the hundreds of Canadian law-enforcement officers who have found themselves in harm's way. One thing is certain about all of these peace officers: they displayed amazing courage and never hesitated to make the ultimate sacrifice for their fellow citizens.

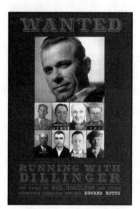

Running With Dillinger
The Story of Red Hamilton and Other Forgotten Canadian Outlaws
978-1-55002-683-2
$24.99

This book picks up where *The Desperate Ones: Canada's Forgotten Outlaws* left off. Here are more remarkable true stories about Canadian crimes and criminals — most of them tales that have been buried for years. The stories begin in colonial Newfoundland, with robbery and murder committed by the notorious Power Gang. As readers travel across the country and through time, they will meet the last two men to be hanged in Prince Edward Island, smugglers who made lake Champlain a battleground, a counterfeiter whose bills were so good they fooled even bank managers, and teenage girls who committed murder in their escape from jail. They will meet the bandits who plundered banks and trains in Eastern Canada and the West, and even the United States. Among them were Same Behan, a robber whose harrowing testimony about the brutal conditions in the Kingston Penittentiary may have brought about his untimely death in "The Hole"; and John "Red" Hamilton, the Canadian-born member of the legendary Dillinger gang.